Walt Disney's Garage of Dreams

Walt Disney's Garage of Dreams

Arthur C. "Buddy" Adler

with additional historical content by Jim Korkis

Foreword by Bob Bowman

Theme Park Press

Theme Park Press publishes its books in a variety of print and electronic formats. Some content that appears in one format may not appear in another.

Editor: Bob McLain
Layout: Artisanal Text

ISBN 979-8-89609-008-3
Printed in the United States of America

Theme Park Press | **www.ThemeParkPress.com**
Address queries to ben@themeparkpress.com

Contents

Foreword ix

Introduction: As I Remember It xi

Part One: Walt Disney's Garage of Dreams 1

  1 Uncle Robert and His Garage 3

  2 The Famous Garage Auction 11

  3 Disney Archivist Dave Smith Begs to Differ 17

  4 The Real Role of Paul Maher 21

  5 The Old Garage Nobody Wanted 25

  6 Garden Grove: Where Dreams Come True 29

  7 The Deed of Gift 33

  8 Dedication Day in Heritage Park 35

  9 Wood Slivers from Walt's Garage 39

10 Walt Disney Recognition Day 43

Part Two: Working for the Mouse 49

11 Hi-Diddle-Dee-Dee, a Contract
   Administrator's Life for Me 51

12 Other Memories of Working at Disney 65

13 Shields and Yarnell and Adler:
   Christmas at Disney World (1978) 69

14 Meeting Celebrities at Disney 73

15 RCID 77

16 It Takes People 79

17 Bob Bowman: My Dance with Disney, 1971–1996 85

18 Bob Penfield: The Last Original Disneyland
   Cast Member 91

19 Paul Mullee: My Boss 95

20 Walt Disney and Me   105

21 Now It's Time to Say Goodbye!   107

Extra: Proclamation for Walt Disney Recognition Day   111

Extra: Walt Disney's Secret Speech   113

A Final Word   119

A Note from Jim Korkis   121

Selected Bibliography   123

About the Author   125

About the Publisher   131

More Books from Theme Park Press   133

Foreword

I became aware of my friend Arthur C. (Buddy) Adler when I was a purchasing director with Disney. Most folks referred to him as either Art, or Buddy if you grew up with him in New Jersey. Sadly, as I write this foreword, Art passed away on September 23, 2014, at the age of 82.

Art will always be remembered in various and different ways. As someone who grew up and loved his hometown of High Bridge, New Jersey, he often reminisced about the early years of his life there and wrote articles about it. Others, like me, knew Art from his Disney days during which he became somewhat famous for his compulsion of saving Walt Disney's Garage. In recent years, Art and I would email each other, talk on the phone, have lunch occasionally, and talk about world affairs. My last conversation with him was on September 19, 2014, as he was struggling to recover from surgery.

In this book, you will witness the selfless acts of one person, one voice, with a strong constitution that allowed him to bring together a group of folks to save this valuable treasure, Walt Disney's Garage.

Art was the kind of person who took "No" as a challenge. He always found a way, whether you liked his approach or not, to accomplish a task he felt important. He was strict to the written word, maybe even to a fault, but he never gave up, NEVER.

And so what you will read and witness in this book is truly a "One Man's Dream", normally associated as a tribute to Walt Disney himself. Enjoy it, talk about it, make sure others know about it, and put yourself in his shoes as you marvel at the perseverance of this one man.

For all those who loved Art for who he was, this is his gift to you. May you rest in peace, my dear friend Art Adler. Heaven has been waiting for you!

Bob Bowman
Retired Vice President, Merchandising
Walt Disney Attractions
September 2014

Introduction: As I Remember It

Everyone has their own opinion or memory about what happened in these stories I am about to share.

Let them write their own book!

This is my book and this is the way I remember it all happening. That's the way I am going to tell these stories. These are the true stories and this is the only place where you can read them. I was there and I saw what I saw and heard what I heard.

In March 1982, when I was living in Laguna Hills, California, and working as a senior contract administrator for Disneyland, I first heard about Walt's garage coming up for auction. It was mentioned in a brief report on a local news station. Had I not been watching, this book never would have been written, my life would have been different, and Walt's garage might have ceased to exist.

I called the television station to confirm what I had just heard. It was true. I could not believe that the Disney organization, my employers, would allow such a historic structure to be auctioned off!

How could Walt's garage have been sitting there quietly for all those many years, weather-beaten and lonely, just waiting for someone to notice? Why wasn't it in a place of honor at Disneyland or in Burbank? Now that people knew it still existed and where it was, would it fall victim to vandals or those hoping to turn a profit by peeling away bits of that historic structure and putting them up for sale?

Even if the garage did sell at the auction, would the buyer it treat it with respect? Would the Disney Company swoop in at the last moment and rescue it?

And how the heck did this guy I had never heard of become the current owner of the garage? Was he a man of integrity and vision? Or was he just out to make a quick buck?

All these questions and so many more troubled me, so I went to the auction.

The clock kept ticking and ticking. I could feel my heart racing.

What would happen if nobody bid on the garage?

The answer, it turned out, was the beginning of one of my most exciting and satisfying adventures.

Let me tell you all about it. This is the way it really happened.

Part One

Walt Disney's Garage of Dreams

One

Uncle Robert and His Garage

After the bankruptcy of Walt's Laugh-O-gram animation studio in Kansas City, Missouri, Walt left the city in late July 1923 on the Santa Fe California Limited. He arrived in Los Angeles in early August 1923. He was twenty-one years old with a pasteboard suitcase.

In an interview later in life, Walt said in the suitcase was everything he owned: "a two-year-old suit of clothes, a sweater, an extra shirt, a lot of drawing materials," and a reel of the cartoon short *Alice's Wonderland* to use as a sample to get some work. He had forty dollars cash in his pocket, all the money he had left after purchasing a first-class train ticket.

Alice's Wonderland was a cartoon short with a young live-action girl portrayed by six-year-old Virginia Davis interacting with cartoon animals in a cartoon background.

Walt moved in with his uncle, Robert Samuel Disney. Robert had moved to California after his retirement a few years earlier. Sixty-two-year-old Robert, born in 1861, was Elias Disney's younger brother by two-and-a-half years.

Walt's father, Elias, never seemed to make much of a success at any endeavor he attempted, from managing a central Florida hotel to farming in Marceline, Missouri, to investing in a jelly factory.

Robert, however, became very successful dabbling in real estate, among other investments. He had owned several hundred acres of farmland a mile from Marceline, which is one of the reasons his older brother Elias decided to move there with his family. The locals didn't care much for Robert who, whenever he showed up to check on his land, behaved in a condescending and authoritative manner, even to his older brother.

He was a physically stout man who enjoyed smoking cigars and was even known to keep one in his mouth when his Vandyke beard was being trimmed.

Robert was living with his second wife, Charlotte, whom he had married in 1921 and who has been described as very strict. She was thirty-two years his junior and five months pregnant with their son, Robert Samuel Disney Jr. She was definitely not as fond or supportive of Walt as Robert's first wife, Margaret, who actively encouraged him to draw by supplying him with material like paper and colored pencils.

They lived in a comfortable little house at 4406 Kingswell Avenue in the Los Feliz section, roughly two-and-a-half miles from the heart of Hollywood. On the side of the house was a small wooden garage.

Robert, ever the businessman, charged his nephew five dollars a week rent. Often that rent was paid by Walt's older brother, Roy O. Disney, who was recuperating from tuberculosis at a veteran's hospital in nearby Sawtelle and receiving a government pension.

Walt was fed up with animation, feeling that audiences had grown tired of the trick of cartoon figures moving about on the screen. All the animation studios were in New York. Walt came to California not only to be with his brother but to try to get into live-action films as a director.

Instead of looking for a regular job, Walt bluffed his way onto studio lots like Universal, Paramount, MGM, and Vitagraph, watching movies being filmed all day. He hoped he could somehow find a job, any job, working at a motion picture studio.

He spent all of August and some of September searching for this job, while increasingly frustrating his uncle Robert and his brother Roy, who both felt that there were plenty of non-movie jobs that would hire Walt and provide him with a steady income. They both nagged at him to do so.

Instead, Walt followed up with Margaret Winkler in New York who was distributing Max Fleischer's *Out of the Inkwell* and Pat Sullivan's *Felix the Cat* cartoon series for theaters. He had contacted her earlier and hoped she would be interested in taking on his *Alice* series.

Winkler had formed her distribution company in February 1922 and was twenty-eight years old. She identified herself as "M.J. Winkler" to disguise that she was a woman. In early September, Walt made arrangements for her to view *Alice's Wonderland* after she expressed some interest.

Finally admitting that he wasn't able to break into the motion picture business in any capacity, Walt once again turned to cartooning.

Walt bought an old used camera that was not in the best of shape for $200 from a local Los Angeles camera shop. Roy had given Walt ten dollars to make up some business cards and letterhead paper proclaiming "Walt Disney, Cartoonist" and using Uncle Robert's address.

He asked Uncle Robert if he could set up his studio in the garage. While Robert was glad that Walt was doing something other than dreaming, he still charged him an extra dollar a week to use the garage.

Walt had to tear apart dry-goods boxes and find spare lumber to build a very crude set-up. The equipment would not accommodate anything more complicated than the simplest of animation.

Walt went to see Alexander Pantages who owned a theater named after him, the Pantages, in downtown Los Angeles. He pitched the idea of doing a series of short joke reels like the ones he had done for the Newman Laugh-O-grams.

In 1921, at the age of nineteen, Walt had done a series of short twenty-five-second animated films that focused on topical humor like ladies' fashions, street repair service, and police corruption. These were produced for Frank Newman,who had a chain of three theaters and were part of the weekly newsreel.

He envisioned a similar series covering the topics of the day but promoting Pantages as well. Just like in a comic strip, when the characters "talked" in this silent cartoon, a balloon filled with written words would appear over their heads. Walt made these every week for a few months.

He was working on this project, doing all the animation himself as stick figures, when he heard back from Winkler with a firm offer for the *Alice* series. On October 16, 1923, Walt and Roy signed a contract with M.J. Winkler for six *Alice Comedies* with an option for two more. Eventually, the Disney Brothers Studio produced fifty-seven *Alice Comedies*.

Realizing he could not operate a full studio out of Uncle Robert's garage, Walt walked up the street two or three blocks to a local realty office called Holly-Vermont Realty at 4651 Kingswell Avenue. The Holly part meant it specialized in Hollywood real estate and Vermont was the street just around the corner.

The owners charged young Walt ten dollars a month for a small room at the rear of the building.

In February 1924, the Disney Brothers Studio moved next door to a larger location at 4649 Kingswell and put their sign out front.

(Much later, that location became a photocopy shop with a sign on one wall declaring it to be Walt Disney's first studio and several Disney photos and artwork pinned up as well.)

From there, the Disney brothers would move to the famous Hyperion Studio in 1926 and then in 1940 to Burbank.

Diane Disney Miller interviewed her father about his life for her book, *The Story of Walt Disney* (Henry Holt, 1957). Many of the things her dad shared with her have never appeared in any other biographies about Walt.

Before her untimely passing in 2013, Mrs. Miller gave me permission to share the following excerpt from her book. It is used here for historical purposes so that readers can better understand why the garage should be considered Walt's first Hollywood studio and gain a clearer idea of the relationship between Uncle Robert and Walt.

Here is how her dad described that time in his career when he decided to get back into animation:

> [Walt Disney] got out his cartoon materials, rented a battered camera and built a camera stand of dry-goods boxes and spare lumber he'd found in his Uncle Robert's garage.
>
> This period in Hollywood reinforced Father's natural inclination to be a self-starter. Instead of crying the blues, he thought of the idea of selling joke reels to Alexander Pantages, who owned a string of Pacific Coast movie and vaudeville theaters.
>
> What he hoped to sell Pantages was basically the same thing he'd sold the Newman Theaters back in Kansas City. He hung around the Pantages office with his idea until he waylaid an assistant, but when he told the assistant about his idea, that assistant said with a bored air, "I'm afraid Mr. Pantages wouldn't be interested."
>
> Just then a voice from another office boomed, "How do you know I wouldn't?" That voice belonged to Mr. Pantages.
>
> Father says that he can still remember the sick look that came over the assistant's face. Even more important, he remembers the lesson the incident taught him. It's this: if you can get to the top man you always have a better chance than you have with the small fry.
>
> When Pantages came out and introduced himself, Father explained his notion. "I think you have a good idea," Pantages told him. "Make up a sample and if it's all you describe, you've got a deal."
>
> So, Father started to run up a joke reel especially for Pantages. He used what he calls "my little stick figures" and combined them with

jokes. He'd draw a head, a mouth and eyes; the body that went with these sketchy anatomical details was a simple collection of single lines. "The best way I can describe these is to say that they looked like white matchsticks on a black background," he told me.

The device was used, primarily, to save him time, but it served his purpose. His stick figures were made to act as if they were telling each other a joke. Then the joke appeared above them in type. The setting was also simplified—a moon in the sky, a tree under which his stick characters walked. The big thing was to cut details so he could do all the work himself.

Father still had the sample *Alice's Wonderland* reel he'd made in Kansas City and was trying to sell it as a series. Ironically, just about the time Father was ready to audition the sample he'd made for Pantages which would have given him enough money to live on if Pantages had okayed it and had ordered more, a New York distributor made him an offer for his cartoon, *Alice's Wonderland.*

The sample for Pantages was completely forgotten. Father hurried out to see Uncle Roy in the hospital. Although he was getting only eighty-five dollars a month from the government, Uncle Roy had been giving Father money to support himself while he made the sample joke reel for Pantages. Financing this new enterprise was a hard decision for him to make. In the end, he grinned at Father and said, "Let's go, Walt."

Their plan was to borrow $500 from Great-Uncle Robert. Father thought that they'd need that much working capital, but borrowing $500 from Great-Uncle Robert wouldn't be easy, they knew. Father and his uncle had had an argument or two.

"He demanded a lot of respect and he didn't think I gave it to him," Father tells me. "Our first argument was about how I'd come West. As everyone knows, the Santa Fe Railroad is really the Atchison, Topeka and Santa Fe Railroad. When I arrived, Uncle Robert asked, 'Did you come through Topeka?' I said, 'I didn't go through Topeka.' 'If you came on the Santa Fe, you did,' he said.

"'Not the train I was on,' I said. 'It bypassed Topeka.'

"Uncle Robert got hot under the collar at that but I wouldn't give in. He had his wife call up the Santa Fe and when he found out that the train on which I'd arrived hadn't gone through Topeka, he was sore at me for weeks."

Great-Uncle Robert was mad at Father about something else, too. In Kansas City, when he was broke, Father had borrowed sixty dollars from his brother Raymond [to invest in the Laugh-O-gram studio], and after that Raymond kept after him to pay that money back. Christmas came and Roy wrote to Father from California, "We're all putting in to buy Mother a vacuum cleaner. I'll put in for you. You get Ray to put in his part."

When Father called Ray, he told him, "You put in for me. After all, you owe me sixty bucks." So Father wrote Roy and said, "I guess we'd better skip Raymond. We'll buy it ourselves."

That wasn't the end of it. When Father came to Los Angeles, Great-Uncle Robert had heard that he still owed Uncle Raymond money. So when Uncle Roy went to Great-Uncle Robert to borrow $500, Great-Uncle Robert said, "No, Walter doesn't pay his debts."

That made Uncle Roy angry. He almost said, "We don't want your five hundred." He thought better of it, however, and in the end, Great-Uncle Robert came through. But when Uncle Roy came back with the check, he told Father, "We're going to pay him back with the very first five hundred we take in."

"Uncle Robert meant well," Father told me. "It was just that he was kind of pompous." Knowing Father, I know he doesn't want me to play up anyone as a villain in this story.

In order to make *The Alice Comedies*, Father rented a place in the rear-end of a real estate office and set up a little studio there.

Roy O. Disney married his wife, Edna Francis, at Uncle Robert's house on April 7, 1925. Home movies were taken and there is a glimpse of the garage in the background.

The $500 loan from Robert Disney was repaid in full on January 12, 1924 (with the second check the Disney brothers received from Winkler), along with the eight-percent interest that Robert had insisted on, for a total of $528.66.

Robert Disney remained obstinate for his entire life. In a letter to his parents dated October 20, 1931, Roy O. Disney wrote about how Robert was upset that Walt had not invited him to come see his new house. Walt had responded that Robert and his family had never visited him at his old house so why should he invite them to his new one. Roy wrote:

Uncle Robert is still as rabid on politics as ever. I "dared" not to agree with him the other night on some of his views and a clash almost ensued. In fact, we had to go to our car escorted by only Aunt Charlotte and Robert Jr., big Robert peevishly walking away from us.

Walt made the comment here not long ago, after a little disagreement with me: "Us Disneys are the most peevish sort of people in the world, always taking offense at each other for something."

Robert Disney died on July 28, 1953, at the age of ninety-one, having seen that Walt was not just a lazy, unreliable dreamer but a do-er. He missed seeing one of Walt's greatest triumphs, Disneyland, by only two years.

For the next thirty years, the little garage remained virtually untouched.

Two

The Famous Garage Auction

After I heard on local television in Laguna Hills, California, about Walt's garage going up on the chopping block, I decided that I had to be at the auction, if only just to see and maybe touch the garage. I wanted to discover why this historic American landmark was sitting there next to a house in Los Angeles rotting away and not on Disneyland's Main Street, U.S.A. for the world to see what one man could accomplish from such humble beginnings.

I arrived deliberately early and, as it turned out, I was the first one to sign the attendance register that day. I wrote my name big. People would know that I had been there. I didn't have $10,000, but I felt I needed to be there just the same.

Before talking to anyone, I darted to the old garage on the side of the house at the back end of the driveway. It was sitting there quietly and humbly. There was nothing to attract any special attention.

I know some people looked and just saw an old garage, even if it were historically significant.

I looked and I saw where Walt began his meteoric rise to making magic for so many people. This was where it all began...where the dreams became a reality.

Physically, the garage looked like a big, plain box measuring twelve feet by eighteen feet by eight feet high. It had a pitched roof with tar paper shingles and a large double front door. It seemed timeless in the sense that it represented no particular architectural period or design.

Inside is what I really wanted to see and touch with the hope that some of Walt's good karma would rub off on me. And, to my surprise, the inside of the garage had never been painted. The karma was intact, as far as I was concerned.

These were the walls that Walt touched and his every breath was captured in the wood. I imagined Walt standing there, looking at those walls, his mind racing as to how to convert it into an animation studio.

I went inside the house and looked over the other items to be auctioned off. There were television and radio reporters all over the place. The publicity had worked and they all hoped for a great story.

One of them even interviewed me when he saw me wearing my Disney name tag. He obviously thought I was there in some official capacity to bid on the garage and was disappointed to find out that I was just an interested fan. There was no representative there from the Disney Company.

I gave several other interviews that day before the auction of the garage, and that night I saw one of them on television.

I talked with Paul Maher, trying to make some sense out of why he would auction off such an important part of Disney history. To this day, I don't think he ever fully understood why the garage was so important.

Finally, near the end of the day, Jay Stewart, the announcer for the television game show *Let's Make a Deal*, assumed the role of auctioneer and enthusiastically tried to get the crowd of about a hundred people excited about bidding on the garage.

The opening bid was set at $10,000.

No one bid. No one offered a counter bid. I could see the light of expectation go out of Maher's eyes.

The television and radio crews packed up almost immediately and left. There was no story here.

A few remaining people milled about the area. I stood there thinking to myself about what would happen now.

Would the garage be used for firewood or made into a coffee table top? At best, it would be ripped apart so that the landlord could continue with her renovations by putting in a new garage.

I knew I had to do something.

I began talking to total strangers about joining me in some sort of coalition and making a bona fide offer to Maher. One of them loudly agreed.

That first person I approached cold turkey was Larry Clardy, a struggling actor. I made my pitch to him about preserving and sharing the historical garage.

Some of the people I approached turned out to be Disney Cast Members from divisions such as WED and MAPO in the Burbank area.

Between Larry and I, we got four people willing to put in enough money so we could present a purchase promise right there and then for $8500. Maher not only accepted my offer, but he and a female friend also became partners. Jay Stewart became another partner.

About a month later at our first meeting, I came up with the name, The Friends of Walt Disney for our group. I was the first chairman and wrote the by-laws. We shortly expanded into eighteen partners.

To make it easier on each of us financially, I divided the $8500 by $500 and came up with seventeen. The original group agreed to bring in others and we finally had eighteen partners with seventeen votes because two of the partners each came in with $250 and therefore had to vote as one.

(Although there were eighteen partners, the list includes twenty-four names. A single partner might include a husband and a wife pairing or two friends.)

Here is the complete list of The Friends of Walt Disney in the order in which they each became a partner:

- Arthur "Buddy" Adler
- Robert Richard and Lawdra Colley
- Larry Clardy
- Jay Stewart
- Kay Armour
- Marian N. Gibbons
- Paul Maher
- Larry and Irene Oppen
- James and Patricia Korecky
- Philip and Billie Hofstee
- Robert Russell
- Lorraine and Linda Colley
- William E. Howard
- John Michael and Gloria P. White
- Susan Heyer
- Steve Granich
- Bobby Sherman
- Valerie Philbrick

Yes, one of those new partners was performer Bobby Sherman. He had been a teen idol in the 1960s and 1970s and had a huge love for

Disney. He built a one-fifth scale model of Disneyland's Main Street U.S.A. by hand for his backyard. It took him two and a half years and $15,000 to build it so that his two young sons could enjoy a bit of the Disney magic with their dad.

One of the first people to see the completed miniature was Walt's daughter, Diane Disney Miller, who exclaimed, "My father would have fallen in love with this!"

On the other hand, Sherman's wife said she was often on the verge of killing him because of the constant hammering.

Later, Sherman was in contact with Tokyo Disneyland to find if they had any interest in having the garage. I strongly urged him not to pursue that option because I didn't want the garage to leave American soil.

As a group, we periodically met at different locations, including Sherman's house which was an enjoyable and memorable experience for everyone.

I was the first chairman. Valerie Philbrick, who worked at Disney, became the second chairman after my year was up. Jay Stewart handled publicity. Larry Open was in charge of public relations. Even though Valerie was officially the chairman, I continued to perform most of those functions.

Other people volunteered their services to help us, including animation legend Hugh Harman who had worked with Walt Disney in the age of silent cartoons. He agreed to supply background information once the garage was on display.

Purchasing the garage was one thing, but the owner was anxious to go on with renovations and get income from her property, so we had to remove it quickly.

I took time to really study the structure and drew up plans. The very first thing I had to do was to make match-marked drawings of the various sections of the garage prior to placing it in storage.

I also had to obtain insurance until I could find a permanent home for this historic structure. I broke the garage down into two side panels, one front and one rear panel, and two front door sections. We removed as many of the roof boards as possible intact, and the work bench panels inside.

Any wood that had splintered off due to weathering over the previous decades, or during out dismantling of the structure, I picked up and placed in two cartons that I kept in my storage unit for years.

It is important to note that these pieces of wood were so tiny that they could never be used again when the garage was re-constructed at its new site. I picked up every piece of wood the moment it fell or broke off, especially at ground level.

Wood that broke off or was too deteriorated to salvage was replaced by new lumber, but by and large more than 97% of the garage was saved! The roof panels would require new asphalt shingles.

Once we had the completed legal bill of sale in our possession on March 26, I looked for a contractor to remove the garage for us. I found William E. Howard and made him a partner in the group in lieu of him receiving payment for his services.

When the garage was finally placed in storage in a weatherproof warehouse in South Gate, The Friends of Walt Disney began to meet as a group to discuss the possibilities for a permanent home. The basic idea, as stated in our by-laws, was that we wanted to donate the garage free and clear to some deserving organization for display to the general public.

Every partner was equal, so all votes had to be unanimous.

We were not all in agreement and there were many differing ideas as to how we would handle the garage. One partner even advocated selling it to recover our costs plus a tidy profit.

He soon became no longer a partner. I bought him out with my own money just to get rid of him and his name will not be mentioned.

I was aghast! I wanted the garage to be put someplace where the public would be able to enjoy it. I know the other partners felt the same way. We did not purchase it to make money but to make magic.

Imagine my surprise when I soon found out that no one wanted Walt's garage!

Three

Disney Archivist
Dave Smith Begs to Differ

Disney Archivist Dave Smith started the Disney Archives at the Burbank Studio on June 22, 1970. It became the model for other corporate archives.

He compiled, organized, and maintained tons of Disney documentation and was regarded as the ultimate authority on all things Disney.

He retired after forty years of preserving Disney history in 2010. At that time, he said:

> Disney is a company among all others I think that re-uses its past all the time. We're constantly looking back into things we did many years ago and using them for our current projects.
>
> The people that worked on the early projects, they're not around anymore so the current company, the various departments have to come to the archives to get their answers and I think that's why we're very important to the company.

I felt it wise to have some sort of official verification that the garage we had purchased was indeed Walt's first studio in Hollywood, so I contacted Dave. He explained to me why the Disney Company had not bid on the garage or was eager to display it at Disneyland. The Disney Company did not consider the garage to be Walt's first studio.

According to Disney history, the Disney Studio did not start until October 16, 1923, when the contract to produce *The Alice Comedies* for M.J. Winkler was signed by Walt and Roy. At that time, the brothers were already working out of the back of a real estate company.

Officially, the Disney Company considers Walt's first studio to be the one down the street from his uncle's house, but that doesn't matter. He may not have done a lot of work in the garage or completed any project that he sold, but this is where he started—and that's what counts.

It was important to me that this garage be preserved so children can look at the humble beginnings of a man who would later create an empire that brought happiness and joy to children all over the world.

It's a way to tell kids that you can start from nothing and, in a relatively short time, achieve great things. I've been a fan of Walt Disney since I was a kid. Heck, I'm still a kid, only a little older and a little grayer. I was just tickled to death about this whole thing… and still am.

Dave Smith was kind enough to write me a letter of verification that I used when I approached various locations about displaying the garage. Here it is:

> Walt Disney Archives
> 500 So. Buena Vista St.
> Burbank, California 91521
>
> March 22, 1982
>
> Mr. Art Adler
>
> Disneyland—Purchasing Contract Adm.
>
> Dear Art:
>
> Walt Disney came to Hollywood in July 1923, to try and find a job in the movie industry. When he had no luck, he decided to try cartoons again. He was rooming with his uncle, Robert Disney, at 4406 Kingswell Ave., at the time.
>
> From an interview:
>
> Walt: When things began to look hopeless, I then got my cartoon thing out again. And I built myself a cartoon stand out of plywood boxes and any lumber I could pick up somewhere….
>
> Interviewer: Were you living with your uncle then?
>
> Walt: Yes. And I built it right down there in the garage. He let me use his garage.
>
> While his *Alice's Wonderland* "pilot" film was making the rounds of distributors in the East, Walt tried to interest Pantages in a weekly joke reel similar to what he had done for the Newman Theater in Kansas City. He did some preliminary work on a reel, probably in the garage, but word came on the purchase of a series of *Alice Comedies*, so the Pantages reel was never finished.
>
> Walt moved down the street on October 8, 1923, to 4651 Kingswell, and there in the back of a real estate office set up the first Disney

Studio. A contract was signed for the *Alice Comedies* on October 16, 1923, the official date of the beginning of the Disney Studio.

Walt only lived with his uncle for a few months.

The garage is the one pictured in Christopher Finch's *The Art of Walt Disney* (Abrams, 1973), page 36, and its brief significance is detailed in the text.

Sincerely yours,

David R. Smith

Archivist

It still makes me smile today that many books as well as internal Disney publications acknowledge the garage as Walt's first studio despite the official policy of the Disney Company.

For example, page 17 of *Your Role in the Disneyland Show*, a Disneyland employee booklet from the 1980s, states: "Walt Disney's new film company had an inauspicious beginning in the corner of an uncle's not-so-new garage in 1923 (picture far left)."

And in 2014 I watched with interest and amusement a Cadillac CTS Sedan television commercial, "Garages", narrated by Neal McDonough. It made the point that many business empires, including Hewlett-Packard, Amazon, Mattel, the Wright Brothers…and even Disney, had all started in a garage.

I thought they did a good job of recreating Walt's garage for the commercial. The house used in the ad is located about a mile north of Robert Disney's actual home, but it is also a Los Feliz dwelling at 2223 Nella Vista Avenue.

I was probably the only one who noticed that the plank wood doors of the real structure are positioned on the left-hand side, while the doors on the garage in the commercial are on the right. But they did use the right street address on the house, 4406.

Whatever the Disney Company officially says, I think we all know Walt's California career started in a tiny garage—a tiny garage that in 1982 needed saving after surviving all alone for over sixty years.

Four

The Real Role of Paul Maher

I often get asked about Paul Maher and his part in saving Walt's garage. In the past, it always made me mad to talk about him because some people give him much too much credit for the whole thing.

My personal feeling, which I still feel strongly today, is that he did not have the passion and vision for Walt's garage that I did. But he is a part of the story, and it would be dishonest not to include him.

So, as Joe Friday used to say on the *Dragnet* television series, I am going to stick to just the facts, ma'am.

If not for Paul Maher, I would not have known that Walt's garage was still around and in need of saving. I give him credit for that.

Paul Maher was born in Whittier, California, in 1952. At the age of twelve, he snuck past security guards and got a chance to get Walt Disney's autograph at the Rose Parade event where Walt was Grand Marshal.

As a young man, he did puppetry and got a job at Knott's Berry Farm and elsewhere doing puppet shows. He later worked as a mime and a Charlie Chaplin impersonator at Universal Studios Hollywood.

In 1978, he started work at Hanna-Barbera as their archivist and researcher.

Dave Smith once told me they did not want to hire Disney fans to work in the Disney Archives because they get overexcited and overzealous about the material and would lose focus on the job they were supposed to be doing. There was even the handful of incidents where employees stole material to "rescue and protect" it.

With Maher's obsession on children's shows, he apparently overstepped some boundaries and displeased Bill Hanna, one of the owners of the studio, with his actions and was terminated.

For his entire life, he collected memorabilia from children's shows in hopes of creating a museum dedicated to children's television. He often spent money he didn't have to acquire these treasures.

He wasn't focused on Disney primarily and at one time had what was called by Tom Hake, owner of the well-known Hake's Americana and Collectibles, the largest collection of Flintstones memorabilia in the world. He also had collections of Casper the Friendly Ghost, Batman, Dick Tracy, and countless other pop culture characters.

In 1981, he went to work as a cartoonist and personal assistant to Walter Lantz, the creator of Woody Woodpecker. He helped Lantz and his wife with personal appearances and with organizing and cataloging all the material Lantz had in storage.

That same year, Paul Maher was looking at slides of historical landmarks with a friend who was a photographer and historian of early Los Angeles when he saw a picture of Uncle Robert's garage.

He didn't recognize it. He was told that it was Walt Disney's first studio and that it was nearby. He told the people in the room that he was going to get that garage, and they looked at him as if he was crazy.

At six a.m. the next day, Maher found the famous garage.

"There were weeds and garbage around the old California home," he later told reporters. "The garbage made it even more fascinating and I had to creep around to the back to find the garage. Like so many fans, I just had to go up and touch it."

Maher found out from a workman that the small one-car garage was planned to be demolished. Maher located the owner, an Asian woman who had no knowledge of the Disney history of her property. She had bought the house as a source of income and was renovating it for that purpose.

She agreed to sell the garage to Maher for $6400, the cost of building a new garage, but he also had to agree to lease the house. He always said he had to make at least six offers before she finally sold him the garage. In the garage, Maher found Uncle Robert Disney's old lawnmower and it still worked.

Maher knew that he couldn't afford to maintain the lease, but insisted that any renovation of the house be stopped while he stayed there. He wanted to experience the same fireplace that Walt did.

The kitchen and the bathroom had already been renovated. He lived in the home for about a year but ran into the expected financial problems and had to break his lease.

When Disney Archivist Dave Smith was interviewed for the *Santa Ana Register* newspaper on February 4, 1981, he stated that the

Disney Company was aware of Maher and the house, but would not be involved in any way.

"We've never gotten into the business of setting up any shrines or restoring any of Disney's former buildings," he said.

During that year, Maher held parties in the house to show off his massive collection of over ten thousand items in hopes of raising support for his museum, with the highlight of the party being when he took his guests into the garage.

He needed money desperately and felt putting the garage up for sale would bring a lot of publicity and potential buyers. He set a minimum bid of $10,000.

Privately, he told friends that he expected the garage to bring maybe a hundred times that amount and that it would not only pay his debts but raise more than enough for him to start building a physical museum.

His dream was never realized. He continued to sell off his collection piece-by-piece to pay for operations after he suffered an aortic aneurysm. He struggled for the next two decades until he passed away on January 31, 2014.

Those are the facts, but since this is my story, I want to make this part very clear. I fully believe that Maher felt that the garage was just another one of the tens of thousands of collectibles in his collection. It did not have the special meaning it did for me and others.

Talking with him at the auction, he did not seem as interested in saving the garage as he did in selling it for as much as he could get. It didn't make any difference to him who bought it or what they would do with it.

He had decided to have an auction of some of his Lantz and Disney collectibles with Walt's garage as the center piece to draw the greatest number of people to the auction as advertised on local TV.

I knew after meeting Paul that if he did not find a buyer for garage, he would leave it right there and take the loss. That was my gut feeling at the time and it scared me! When the opening bid of $10,000 did not materialize, Paul was faced with a real dilemma until I came to him and made my offer of $8500.

It was only then, when Maher saw that I was so passionate about saving Walt's garage, that he wanted to get on board. He borrowed the money from a friend of his, Marian Gibbons, who had already bought into the garage coalition I had created. She loaned him $500. If not for that nice lady, his name would not even be on the listing of The Friends of Walt Disney!

Now allow me to be clear: Paul was a nice enough fellow and I had no objection to his joining us, but I want the record of his true motives to be clear.

Over the decades, I think he got too much credit for saving Walt's garage when it was really I and The Friends of Walt Disney who did all the work to remove it, store it, and finally find a place where it could be located and shared.

Since everyone had some function in The Friends of Walt Disney, we made him the historian, but I don't remember any contribution he made in that capacity. He didn't actively search for new information about the garage, didn't put together any documentation about how the garage was saved, or anything else.

He spent the rest of his life dreaming of his Children's Television Museum and thought that one day the garage might be part of that physical location, just like all the other collectibles he had acquired over the years.

For me, despite everything else I was doing in my own life, I always made time to keep looking for a permanent home for the garage. It was not just a casual interest. For me, it was a mission and a passion.

I am genuinely sorry that Paul's dream of a museum was never realized. I believe in dreams and I believe in dreams coming true.

When it came to Walt's garage, my dreams eventually came true, but there were many moments of cliff-hanging suspense before they did.

Five

The Old Garage Nobody Wanted

Since The Friends of Walt Disney had partners spread out all over Orange and Los Angeles counties and beyond, we met often enough at some central location to take care of business and keep focused on finding a site for the garage.

I took on most of the hunt to find a permanent home, including following up on all the ideas from the other partners. It was indeed a daunting task and took more time than expected because no one seemed to want the garage.

Most organizations liked the idea of having the garage, especially for free, but they didn't like all the additional expenses connected with such an endeavor. It hadn't even occurred to me that there would be costs like security, insurance, and maintenance.

One option I proposed while we looked for a permanent location was a cross-country tour of shopping malls and fairs.

As we explored that idea, it became clear that one of the problems would be the physical transportation. Excessive movement could have been harmful to the garage's integrity. We never completely ruled out the idea, but decided to pursue other options first.

Naturally, one of the first places I went was to the Disney Studio, where I got an appointment to meet with CEO Card Walker. I had learned from Walt that you should start at the top with the decision-maker.

After Walt Disney died in 1966, Walker became executive vice president and chief operating officer. When Walt's brother Roy O. Disney died in 1971, he became company president, serving under Chairman and CEO Donn Tatum. In November 1976, Walker took over chief executive officer duties from Tatum, and finally in 1980 became chairman of the board upon Tatum's retirement .

Walker himself retired as CEO three years later, in February 1983, but stayed on as chairman until May 1 to oversee the opening of Tokyo Disneyland.

I explained to Card that my idea was to donate the garage free of charge to Disneyland for permanent display in a location of their choice. I wanted it to be a symbol for young people to see what great heights they could achieve from such humble beginnings.

Card liked the idea, but informed me that since it was so deeply connected to Walt that he would have to take it up with the Disney family. I thanked Card and he promised he would get back to me.

About a month or so later, in April, I received a call from Card Walker who told me that he had brought my proposal to the attention of the Disney family. Ron Miller, Walt Disney's son-in-law, had firmly stated that the family did not wish the garage to be on display in any Disney theme park or anywhere else on Disney property.

I told Card that was pretty cold and pretty clear. Card said, "I know and I am sorry."

I think Card was thinking of the garage being put somewhere at the end of Main Street, U.S.A. at Disneyland or at the Disney Studio as a special attraction for visitors.

Years later, I realized why I got such a negative answer. Miller was fighting for his life at the Disney Studio. On September 7, 1984, he was finally forced to tender his resignation, even though he was Walt Disney's son-in-law.

Michael Eisner and Frank Wells took over and everything that Miller had accomplished from The Disney Channel to bringing on new talent like Tim Burton were completely forgotten or erased from the history.

I was also told later that the Disney family, being very private, did not want Walt to become just another character in the parks where he would be a thing on t-shirts and coffee cups and not a real person.

I knew the Disney family never got along well with Eisner after he took over. I also knew it would do no good to keep pressing my case.

I was never given anything in writing on this subject from Card Walker or Ron Dominguez, president of Disneyland, or anyone else, because I feel they did not want any written record of my proposal and rejection.

Now you know the truth about why Walt's first studio never ended up on Disney property.

While I waited for an answer from the Disney Company, I continued to follow up on other possibilities, without success.

On May 31, 1982, I contacted the Department of Parks and Recreation of Los Angeles County, and on June 2 got a response from its director, Ralph S. Cryder, excerpted here:

> The Department of Parks and Recreation for Los Angeles County would be willing to discuss a possible lease agreement with The Friends of Walt Disney relative to the garage being placed on suitable park property through a negotiated lease agreement. Said lease agreement would not necessarily be free of charge, but if the situation is deemed feasible, I am sure a normal fee, as required by law, could be negotiated.
>
> Also the maintenance and security protection to such a structure would be necessary, along with the proper security bond, insurance, etc.
>
> It should also be recognized that such a structure erected on park property would really be of no value unless some mechanism is established to view the facility, which then would require personnel on your part, so that the facility can be supervised throughout the year.

I had no desire to negotiate for a lease that I wouldn't touch with a ten-foot pole. The garage was a gift, for crying out loud. I began to realize that even a free gift would cost The Friends of Walt Disney even more money as costs continued to accumulate for storage and insurance.

On February 17, 1983, I contacted the Smithsonian Institute and the National Museum of American History in Washington, D.C., and on March 4 got this reply from museum representative Carl H. Scheele:

> I am very much interested in your proposal. I must advise you, however, that I have not pursued conversations with my colleagues here far enough to respond with a total commitment. The prospect of obtaining additional memorabilia also interests me.
>
> I should perhaps state immediately that we could not place the garage on exhibit as soon as it arrived. You and your colleagues should be aware of this. We have exhibit commitments already in place in this Museum far into 1985. However, future projections in exhibit planning beyond that date hold some good potential promise.
>
> In addition, we would have to discuss problems such as shipping. I would need to know certain details like the volume of space the building occupies knocked down and the dimensions of the building when erected.
>
> For the moment, please be assured that my interest in acquiring the structure for the Museum's collections is very strong and supportive.

Reading between the lines, it was obvious this was another dead end. Having Walt's garage unavailable for viewing by the public would defeat the purpose of rescuing it.

Sometime later, I received a telephone call from Mr. Scheele and he stated that, among other things, we would have to at least pay for the full shipping in accordance with their instructions.

There would be no guarantee when the garage would be placed on display for the general public or for how long, and once removed from display when and if it would ever be displayed again.

I thanked him but I just knew we could get a better offer.

I went to the Burbank Historical Society and, while they were initially enthusiastic, received this response from their president, Charles Lovejoy, on March 23, 1983:

> I am sorry for the delay in writing to you. I did have a letter written to you but I had to change it. It was necessary for us to confer with the Burbank Parks and Recreation Department in order to O.K. your garage.
>
> To our chagrin, the Department has rejected our plan to incorporate your building into our complex. I must inform you that we are going to have to reject your plan. Thank you for your time and effort.

Thanks for nothing, I thought. Burbank was Walt's "other home". It was where his studio still operated. It was where he first wanted to build Disneyland. The garage should be in Burbank or Anaheim. I was getting very frustrated.

I contacted historical societies in Anaheim and Orange County to no response. I contacted the Hart Ranch and Museum in Corona, California, the former home of silent movie cowboy star William S. Hart that displayed historical structures, and they had no interest.

Neither did Heritage Square in Los Angeles or The Los Angeles Museum of Natural History or the Lasky-DeMille Barn that became the home of the Hollywood Heritage Museum or even Universal Studios Hollywood.

In the case of the Los Angeles City Parks, I was told that there was too great a risk for vandalism of the site and that they were not in a position to provide around-the-clock protection or a security fence.

It seemed I had pretty much run out of places to approach. But, like a good Disney film, just as it got darkest for the hero, there was a shining light and a happy ending. It just never occurred to me that the light would be coming just two miles from Disneyland.

Six

Garden Grove: Where Dreams Come True

One day while driving around Euclid Avenue in Garden Grove, California, I noticed a sign that said "Heritage Park". My curiosity got the better of me. I turned around and drove back to take a look, and to my great surprise it turned out to be a collection of local historical buildings that had been relocated to this site.

The Garden Grove Historical Society, a private, non-profit organization that receives no government funding, operated the location.

The property features the Stanley House, built in 1891, and now a museum for displays on the early years of Garden Grove. In 1970, Agnes Stanley donated two acres to the Garden Grove Historical Society, and the property is now known officially as the Stanley Ranch Museum. Some of Garden Grove's oldest homes and business buildings have been moved to this location.

The Stanley House is the focus home at the museum. Also included at the site are other buildings dating from the late 1800s to the early 1900s. Garden Grove's first post office, opened in 1877, stands proudly for people to enjoy, along with the Electric Shoe Shop/Barber Shop and Garden Grove's No. 1 fire engine, a 1926 American La France.

There is an old schoolhouse, an early dentist room, a general store, a barn, and artifacts from the turn of the twentieth century. I may have been hallucinating but I could visualize Walt's first studio feeling right at home here.

Even though the ranch is now surrounded by modern development, when you are standing in the park it doesn't take too much imagination to picture what the city looked like more than a hundred years ago. Near the ranch you can also find Garden Grove's Historic Main Street, which consists of buildings that similarly date back to the turn of the twentieth century.

I had rarely been so excited. It was as if the spirit of Walt himself had guided me here just as I was starting to give up hope. This park represented the time period that Walt loved and on which he based Main Street, U.S.A.

It had the genuine feeling of the "good old days" when Walt was starting off in his garage. And you could see the top of Space Mountain at Disneyland from Heritage Park!

I made an appointment to meet with the president of Heritage Park, Terry B. Thomas, to make my proposal to him. Terry turned out to be a really great fellow who understood my intentions and shared my interest in them.

He assured me that he would bring the issue up at the next board meeting. I knew that we would get along just fine and we did—even up to today! Terry was a man of his word and brought my proposal to the board of directors, where it was enthusiastically accepted.

Here is that memorable letter:

> Heritage Park
>
> September 15, 1983
>
> Dear Mr. Adler:
>
> At the August and September Board Meeting of the Garden Grove Historical Society, the offer of the Walt Disney Studio Garage was presented, discussed and accepted by the Board Members present.
>
> The acceptance was based on the following general conditions. Any differences can be worked out between the Board and The Friends of Walt Disney. Further details can also be worked out if The Friends of Walt Disney are in agreement with our offer.
>
> The Garden Grove Historical will provide space and install a suitable concrete foundation/floor for the Garage. The Friends of Walt Disney will donate the Garage and will reconstruct it on the site at Heritage Park.
>
> The Friends will also donate any suitable material of their choosing to be put on display in the Garage once it is secure. Upkeep and maintenance of both the Garage and the displays will be the responsibility of the Garden Grove Historical Society. Of course, any assistance by The Friends of Walt Disney would be welcome.
>
> In the event that the Garden Grove Historical Society ceases to exist or disposes of the property at Heritage Park, the Walt Disney Studio Garage and related contents will be returned to The Friends of Walt Disney.

The Garden Grove Historical Society will provide a plaque and place it on or at the Garage indicating that the Garage was donated by The Friends of Walt Disney and list the names of the Friends.

The Friends of Walt Disney are welcome to come and visit at any time and discuss any problems or potential arrangements.

Sincerely:

Terry B. Thomas, President

Of course, The Friends of Walt Disney accepted immediately. There was no need for any lengthy discussion. This was what we all wanted. The garage would be displayed properly to the general public in a beautiful setting, just minutes from Disneyland. It would be well taken care of and it would be loved and appreciated.

I donated some of my Disney memorabilia collection which is still in the garage to this day in a long glass case. Everything from old Disneyland ticket books to guide books to stuffed animals to lithographs that hang on the walls. It was something for every generation so people could connect the place with Walt Disney.

While writing these memories and thoughts for this book in mid-2013, I called the Garden Grove Historical Society/Heritage Park in Garden Grove to see if my old friend and former president of that organization, Terry Thomas, was still around. I was happy to find out that he was and we had a great chat on the phone. I was also happy that he was about to become president once again.

What was even greater news was what Terry said next:

Art, I want you to know how much we all appreciate what you and The Friends Of Walt Disney did for us by donating Walt Disney's First Studio in California to us and that in fact it has become the most popular historical structure that we have on our property! It is hard to describe the huge enthusiasm that people have for the place. Many people come specifically just to see it.

Seven

The Deed of Gift

You can't just give something away, even for free, anymore. There are legalities that have to be followed. I prepared the Deed of Gift, and after all the necessary signatures, it was ready in early 1984.

Here is the text of that document:

DEED OF GIFT

The group known as "The Friends of Walt Disney" whose names are individually listed below, declare for and in consideration of the love and affection for the great memory and legacy of Walt Disney, our public spirit, and the desire to preserve the structural integrity of this historical garage known as "Walt Disney's First Studio" formerly located at 4406 Kingswell Avenue, Los Angeles, California, described below, "The Friends of Walt Disney" do hereby donate Walt Disney's First Studio free and clear of any encumbrances whatsoever to The Garden Grove Historical Society, Garden Grove, California, on March 10, 1984. All in accordance with the Garden Grove's Letter of Acceptance dated September 15, 1983.

Description

Walt Disney's First Studio in California is a one (1) story, two (2) door, one (1) window all-wooden structure approximately twelve feet wide by eighteen feet long by ten feet high with Lap boards and a slightly pitched roof. Original purchase price $8,500.00 on March 21, 1982.

The remaining partners of "The Friends of Walt Disney" are listed in the order that each became a partner:

Arthur C. "Buddy" Adler

Robert Richard and Lawdra Colley

Larry Clardy

Jay Stewart

Kay Armour

Marian N. Gibbons

Paul Maher

Larry and Irene Oppen

James and Patricia Korecky

Phillip and Billie Hofstee

Robert Russel, Lorraine, and Linda Colley

William E. Howard

John Michael and Gloria P. White

Susan Meyer

Steve Granich

Bobby Sherman

Valerie Philbrick

The cumulative value of this historical structure including original partnership share purchases, share buyout, insurance, storage fees, dismantling and erection costs, time and effort, travel expenses and appreciation, etc. is $25,000.00 as appraised by The Friends of Walt Disney.

The document was signed Terry Thomas, Valerie Philbrick, Robert Colley (who was at that time treasurer and vice chairman of the group), and me.

Eight

Dedication Day in Heritage Park

The Garden Grove Historical Society had given the outside of the garage a new coat of white primer paint to help protect it against the weather. The garage looked neat and pretty when it finally came time to dedicate it in Heritage Park.

The inside was left untouched so that it was just as it was when Walt was inside it and dreaming of the future.

In March 1984, permits had been obtained and preparations for the foundation slab were underway, and by April 24, 1984, the slab was completed.

Reconstruction of the garage by members of the Historical Society was nearing completion by the end of June. The Friends of Walt Disney had carefully marked the various parts and pieces of the garage when it was dismantled and made a sketch of the building showing how the pieces went together.

During the reconstruction of the roof, however, a problem developed when the parts didn't seem to be going together properly.

After some study and checking the marking and measuring the various sections, it was discovered that the sketch showed the left and right sections backwards and in reverse order. This was corrected and the roof was completed and new roofing material installed.

We had replaced any necessary wood before repainting. We placed a plaque listing "The Friends of Walt Disney" on the inside of the right garage door. Others had donated some additional memorabilia to supplement my original donation.

The official dedication of the garage was on October 20, 1984. A yellow ribbon was strung across the doors of the garage that would later be cut as part of the ceremonies by Mickey and Minnie Mouse. (Since I still worked for the Disney Company, I was able to arrange to have a Mickey and Minnie Mouse pair of costumed characters from Disneyland to drop by for the ceremonies.)

The event was open to the public. More than a hundred Disney fans and local officials attended. There was punch, food, and speeches.

Among those attending the dedication was legendary animator and Imagineer Bill Justice, who told the press: "This is a good place for it. Otherwise it might not be appreciated."

We had reporters from the *Los Angeles Times*, the *Orange County Register*, the *Anaheim Bulletin*, *Orange Coast* magazine, and even some Disney publications and Disney fan publications like the *Orange County Passport*, part of the National Fantasy Fan Club organization.

The local U.S. Post Office in Garden Grove came up with a beautiful First Day cover envelope commemorating the event. It featured a picture of The Famous Old Garage on the left side with these words above: Dedication of the First Disney Studio—A Garage Relocated to Heritage Park in Garden Grove, CA.

Below the picture were the words: October 20, 1984. Commemorated by The Garden Grove Historical Society. The cover was cancelled "Garden Grove, Ca., 92640, October 20 PM 1984", and had three cancelled U.S. postage stamps affixed on it: a 6-cent California stamp, a 6-cent Walt Disney stamp, and a 6-cent Missouri stamp (Walt had lived and worked in Missouri before he moved to California).

President of the Garden Grove Historical Society Terry Thomas recently wrote to me:

> In the thirty or so years since the garage was reconstructed and the dedication was held, the primary activity on the garage has been regular maintenance and repair when necessary.
>
> The garage doors had to be reconstructed due to normal aging and it has received a couple of new roofs and several paint jobs. Most of the repainting has been done by members of local Boy Scout troops that are doing a community service project for their Eagle Scout Award. These are done with proper preparation and adult scout leader guidance when necessary and the overall acceptance of the Historical Society.
>
> On one occasion, the garage was in need of a new paint job and two girls from a local high school, looking for a community service project, undertook the project. Under the guidance of a member of the Historical Society, the job was completed and it turned out to be one of the best paint jobs done at the Museum by a non-professional.
>
> The Disney Garage is part of our regular scheduled tours and the special group tours conducted at the museum. It is one of eight buildings currently part of the tour.

From the comments of our tour guests, it is one of our exhibits they most want to visit. We have many school and other youth groups that come and the Disney Garage is high on their list of things that they want to see.

We also have occasional visitors from all over drop by outside of our regular tour hours just to see the garage. We will, if possible, take the time to show it to them.

We were very fortunate to have Art Adler and The Friends of Walt Disney find us in 1983 and agree to have the Disney Garage located at the Stanley Ranch Museum.

It is a very popular attraction and is one of the draws that brings the public to our Museum. The Friends of Walt Disney have gone their separate ways since obtaining the garage but their effort and personal financial investment saved a small but important structure from being demolished and gave it to the Garden Grove Historical Society for the enjoyment of the public for many years to come.

I had a great group of partners in The Friends of Walt Disney whose hearts were in the right place and all contributed in some ways.

We had great meetings at different locations, great discussions, and great ideas. All in all, I would not have traded this experience of doing something good for the community while preserving and celebrating the life of a great American and international icon who brought joy, laughter, and happiness to the world and its children of all ages.

I drop by now and then at Garden Grove to keep an eye on the garage and am always pleased that such great care and attention is being paid to it and that so many people are enjoying it.

You can see it for yourself:

The Stanley Ranch Museum
12174 Euclid Street
Garden Grove, California 92840

714-530-8871
gardengrovehistsoc@att.net

Tell them Buddy sent you! And be sure to touch the inside to get a dose of Walt's karma.

Nine

Wood Slivers from Walt's Garage

When The Friends Of Walt Disney dismantled Walt's garage to place into storage and insure it, pieces of wood along the ground line broke off because it the structure had deteriorated due to weather.

When Walt made use of the garage, it had not been brand new but in existence for some years before Uncle Robert moved in. The pieces that broke off could not be replaced. It was obvious that new wood would be needed in those areas when we would later reconstruct the building.

So, before I left the site at 4406 Kingswell Avenue, I stood there looking at these pieces of wood that broke off and that would be in the trash can later that day. With no real plan in mind, I took two cartons and picked up most of them and placed them in my personal storage unit, just for the sake of not throwing them out.

I kept that wood for roughly twelve years. Every time I went to my storage unit and saw those two boxes of wood I thought to myself, "Throw them out!" But I could never bring myself to do that, because in my gut it would be like tossing history into the garbage.

It was Walt's history, and even though it was taking up space, I just couldn't bring myself to do anything about it.

Finally, an idea crossed my mind to put together some sort of Disney collector business and market the wood scraps. I was sure there were many Walt fans who would like to own a piece of the original studio.

But I had no idea how to start. Over the years, I had purchased collectibles and had been a member of the National Fantasy Fan Club that often had conventions where unique Disney collectibles were sold.

As I thought of ways to do it, it just seemed to be more complicated and time consuming, and I would put the idea aside once again.

Then, one day, I thought of having a friend of mine cut up whatever good wood was part of the weathered, decomposed wood into very small manageable pieces that were 1/4 inch square by 1.5 inches long.

He did and placed a little under 1800 pieces in a plastic bag and gave them to me. Back into my storage unit they went again, for a very long time.

Now whenever I went to my storage unit I would see this plastic bag of wood staring at me and didn't know where to go from this point. Nonetheless, I got myself a post office box in North Hollywood and came up with the name "Historic Memorabilia Ltd."

I had to decide what I could place a wood sliver inside of that would easy to mail or cart around to conventions. I decided to go with a small narrow glass vial with a black plastic screw-on cap. I made that choice because it would be a safe vessel for the wood and would also allow the collector to take out the wood and hold it or examine it, if he chose to do so.

The next item to consider was a certificate that would state authenticity of the item. It took a long time to research and check out printing houses that could print what I conceived as a stock certificate-quality Certificate of Authenticity.

After some time, I found the certificate I preferred and the proper colors and paper type, but they were not cheap. I settled upon a 9-inch by 12-inch certificate that was very colorful with a black-and-gray eagle and scrollwork on it, and a colorful border in several shades of green. They were sequentially numbered with an embossed gold seal at the bottom stating, Walt's Disney's First Studio. Authentic Wood.

The text on the certificate stated:

> This numbered certificate of authenticity certifies that the numbered piece of wood in the glass vial was part of "Walt Disney's First Studio" also known as "The Old Garage" formerly located on the property owned by Walt's Uncle, Robert Disney, at 4406 Kingswell Ave., Los Angeles ,California. "The Old Garage" is referred to in several books on Disney, earlier Disney employee publications as verified by the story of "How Walt Disney's First Studio Was Saved", and "The Old Garage" verified by the Disney Archives in Burbank, California. Arthur C. Adler, President, Historic Memorabilia Ltd.

The certificates were gorgeous and impressive.

Next I had to create peel-off labels that stick to glass for the vials which would say, "Authentic Wood From Walt Disney's First Studio", along with a number that matches the numbers on the Certificate of Authenticity.

I also went to the Disney Studio in Burbank and talked them into giving me an official, black-and-white 8-inch by 10-inch photo of "The Old Garage" taken at 4406 Kingswell Ave. in Los Angeles for the purpose of making good photocopies and including a copy with the collectible package.

The real test of my personal talents was to come up with a "story book," because I did not want any living soul to think that I had saved Walt's first studio only to cut it up in little pieces and sell them.

After all, that was what I was trying to prevent by saving the garage.

Slowly, I put together a booklet of about 30 pages, which included a much shorter and less polished version of the story here, along with copies of newspaper articles and other documents. It was spiral bound with a pastel cover. As the years progressed I continued to improve the quality of the paper and the selection of material inside.

I gave some of these packets away to friends and relatives, made some personal sales, sold some on eBay for a short time, and sold some at National Fantasy Fan Club (now known as the Disneyana Fan Club) conventions and at similar venues.

It finally got too much for me, and so I sold the remaining slivers to the well-known and respected dealer in Disney collectibles, Phil Sears. I saved just a few pieces for myself.

Ten

Walt Disney Recognition Day

After the dedication ceremony, it occurred to me that there was no holiday or day of recognition for Walt Disney. I thought something should be done about it and that 1985 was a particularly opportune time because Disneyland was celebrating its 30th anniversary.

I was sure that this time I could get support from the Disney Company because it would seem to them a wonderful promotional opportunity. Besides, Walt was the sort of man that Congress should be holding up as an example for children.

No one, not the Disney Company, the Disney family, or any Disney fan club, had ever attempted to do persuade the U.S. Congress to set aside a day of recognition for Walt Disney.

It didn't intimidate me. I just had to figure out who I should contact.

At the time, there was one congressman whom I admired greatly for his fiery, no-nonsense approach to serious political issues. His name was Congressman Robert K. "Bob" Dornan (R-Calif) who had a gruff, even terse manner of making his points.

I wrote Bob Dornan a letter and sent it to his California office detailing my idea for a "Walt Disney Recognition Day" to occur on Walt's birthday, December 5.

To my great and joyful surprise, Congressman Dornan loved my idea and thus started a new friendship. Throughout 1984, Dornan kept me posted about his efforts to obtain the backing of other members of the House and Senate for our proposal.

He got thirty co-sponsors in a relatively short time. Eventually, more than half the House of Representatives ended up as co-sponsors.

Around six representatives turned down the opportunity to co-sponsor the bill, not because they disliked the creator of Mickey Mouse and Disneyland, but because they were protesting that Congress spent too much time and money voting on commemorative days and weeks for various people and causes.

At the time, roughly five hundred resolutions were introduced that year for commemorative days—too many to fit into the days of the year! Dornan told me this was not unusual. Lillian Fernandez, then the staff director for the House subcommittee that deal with commemorative holidays, said:

> These laws just express a sentiment. People don't have to go out and celebrate these things. They're good-will legislation and they make a lot of people happy.

I celebrated the first Walt Disney Recognition Day and continued to do so every year.

The Joint Resolution

Here is the text of the joint resolution that was presented and voted on.

99th Congress 1st Session H.J. Res. 377

IN THE HOUSE OF REPRESENTATIVES September 9, 1985

Mr. Dornan of California introduced the following joint resolution, which was referred to the Committee on Post Office and Civil Service

JOINT RESOLUTION

To designate December 5, 1985, as "Walt Disney Recognition Day".

Whereas in 1985 there occurs the 30th anniversary of the founding of Disneyland;

Whereas December 5, 1985, is the 84th anniversary of the birth of the founder of Disneyland, Walter Elias Disney;

Whereas the delightful characters created by Walt Disney, including Mickey Mouse and Donald Duck, have brought joy to several generations;

Whereas Walt Disney used the characters he created to promote family values and to teach civic and moral lessons;

Whereas the unceasing commitment of Walt Disney to excellence led him to perfect animation as an art form;

Whereas Walt Disney produced nature documentaries that yielded fascinating insights into the animal kingdom and emphasized the importance of conserving the natural heritage of the Nation;

Whereas Walt Disney devoted an enormous amount of time and resources to improving the quality of urban life in the United States through the construction of Walt Disney World and Epcot Center;

Whereas classic films produced by Walt Disney included *Fantasia*,

Bambi, and the first full-length animated cartoon, *Snow White and the Seven Dwarfs*; and

Whereas Walt Disney was an American folk hero who became famous worldwide:

Now, therefore, be it

Resolved by the Senate and House of Representatives of the United States of America in Congress assembled, that December 5, 1985, hereby is designated "Walt Disney Recognition Day", and the President of the United States is authorized and requested to issue a proclamation calling upon the people of the United States to observe such day with appropriate ceremonies and activities.

The resolution passed unanimously and without objection on Tuesday, October 3, 1985, at 7:00 p.m. Dornan wrote me a nice letter thanking me for suggesting the idea and for all my support.

He later sent me a copy of the Congressional Record for December 3, 1985. Dornan had asked and was given permission to address the House for one minute to revise and extend his remarks. The following appears on page H 10561:

Mr. Speaker, I want to thank 227 of my colleagues for joining me in co-sponsoring a joint resolution that the President will sign this week to set aside a commemorative day for a truly unique and great American, Walt Elias Disney.

I now have the joy and privilege of representing Disneyland, now celebrating its 30th anniversary, and I especially enjoy taking the older two of my four grandchildren back to relive those wonderful moments that I experienced with my own family, my five children, at Disney World and Disneyland. This American, Walt Disney, from very humble beginnings in the Midwest, probably created more joy for his fellow citizens, particularly our children and grandchildren, than any who has ever lived in this country, indeed the world.

His cartoon characters, Mickey Mouse and Donald Duck, his books, films, records and wildlife series, educational materials, and internationally known theme parks, have made the name Walt Disney immortal and synonymous with joy, good will, and integrity.

I want to particularly thank Arthur 'Buddy' Adler, a wonderful actor and former Disneyland employee, for bringing the suggestion to me for a long-overdue tribute to a man who passed away in 1966 to what I am sure is a great eternal reward. Walt Disney's good works have been recognized worldwide and I believe that it is only proper that we formally recognize Walt Disney's accomplishments.

Thank you for this commemorative to Walt Disney.

Earlier, I had been told to be ready to go on a moment's notice to attend the signing and made airline reservations just to be safe. But when I phoned Washington and talked to Dornan's assistant, Joe Eule, I was told the signing was going to be postponed.

Both President Reagan and Vice President George Bush would be out of town during the time when the bill could be signed. Dornan tried to console me that by delaying the signing for a year there was the great possibility that it could take place in the White House Rose Garden and get more publicity.

In addition, it could be tied in to the 15th anniversary of Walt Disney World in 1986. The Senate had to pass an amended version designating December 5, 1986, as Walt Disney Recognition Day. Reagan assured everyone that he would make himself available for the signing.

Ronald Reagan had been a good friend of Walt Disney even before he got into politics. He was one of the three television hosts for the opening of Disneyland on July 17, 1955.

When he became governor of California, Reagan corresponded with the postmaster general of the United States supporting the release of a commemorative six-cent postage stamp in 1968 honoring Walt Disney. (At least ten years had to pass after an individual's death before they could be considered for a stamp. Reagan must have been very convincing to get an exception so that Walt was honored just two years after his passing.)

When Reagan was elected president of the United States, and Washington, D.C. was too snowed in for his inaugural parade in January, it was held May 27, 1985, in front of Epcot's American Adventure at Walt Disney World. Reagan was brought in by a helicopter that landed behind the American Adventure. The president spoke at 12:41 p.m. from a reviewing stand that resembled a huge plexiglass box in front of the pavilion.

I impatiently waited for a year.

Dornan wrote to me when the proclamation was signed into law by President Reagan:

A ceremony was supposed to be held but due to scheduling conflicts and other factors, it was impossible to hold a formal White House ceremony. The proclamation was officially issued by President Reagan on December 5, 1986.

You can be very proud that your efforts on behalf of Walt Disney have been successful. Your dedication and spirit have proved once again that in America, one man's voice can be heard and heeded in the halls of government.

Thanks again for all your help.

Robert K. Dornan, U.S. Congressman

[To read the text of the proclamation, refer to "Extra: Proclamation for Walt Disney Recognition Day", toward the end of the book.]

When I was interviewed by the newspapers, I stated: "Walt Disney has had an overwhelming presence in my life. I grew up with him."

I received a letter on Walt Disney Attractions letterhead paper a few months later. It was dated March 17, 1987, and was from Richard "Dick" Nunis, who was then the president of the Recreation Division of Walt Disney Attractions, which basically meant that he was in charge of Disneyland and Walt Disney World. He wrote:

Dear Buddy,

First of all, let me say that I apologize that no one wrote to you and complimented you on helping get the recognition for the great man Walt Disney. I would like to thank you because having known Walt I can't think of any man that is more deserving of this recognition!

I wish you the very best of luck on your book, *The Old Garage Nobody Wanted*, and I wish you the very best of luck in the future.

Sincerely, Richard A. Nunis

More people know who Walt Disney and Mickey Mouse are than know who is the president of the United States of America. I wish I would have known Walt, but getting him a national day of recognition and saving his first studio are projects in my life that I will always remember with great joy.

I'm sure Walt Disney is smiling.

Part Two

Working for the Mouse

Eleven

Hi-Diddle-Dee-Dee, a Contract Administrator's Life for Me!

When I tell people I worked for Disney, they immediately assume it must have been in some entertainment capacity, perhaps even slipping on Goofy's huge shoes and walking around Walt Disney World.

Not even close. My job title was senior contract administrator. That may not sound as exciting as operating an attraction or shooting off fireworks every night, but the truth is that Disney is a business, and as such, it needs to have a massive backstage administrative staff to handle business matters so that the show can go on.

A senior contract administrator is equivalent to a salaried manager position. My job was to enforce the corporate purchasing policies and procedures and at the same time set up an efficient system for the Disney Company to work with outside contractors to obtain materials and services that would avoid excessive costs, unprofessional work, and unfairness in the reviewing of bids.

I am sure, for the average Disney fan, that doesn't sound very glamorous.

But did you enjoy the New Fantasyland that opened at Disneyland in 1983? Did you feel safe on the Matterhorn? Were you able to ride on the sailing ship *Columbia* on July 4? Then you are more than welcome.

Here are some excerpts from a few memos and letters sent to me over a three-month period in the summer of 1983:

> WED Enterprises, Dave Melanson June 30,1983: "I would like to thank you for all your efforts in keeping the Fantasyland project in 'LINE' with regards to our contractual commitments. I believe all of our efforts and hard work have paid off by the success of the New Fantasyland."

> Bill Bealer, May 31, 1983: "Thanks for getting the additional planter railings installed by Washington Iron and Ted and Daniels prior to

the Fantasyland opening. The work was done much more quickly than I thought possible. I appreciate your response and help. It wouldn't have happened without your effort."

Ed Winger, July 18,1983: "I would like to take this opportunity to congratulate you on your performance on the Fantasyland '83 project. You are a very dedicated individual with a persistent demand for accuracy and timing. We have not had this in the past. I appreciate your work."

Concrete Cutting International, Edward Hughes, Vice President, July 8, 1983: "We at Concrete Cutting International have dealt with several of your personnel at Disneyland in the capacity of sub-contractor for several years. During the past year and a half, we have dealt primarily with Art Adler. We have found Art to be personable, fair, and honest, and unlike many of our accounts, he is available to help us when we need answers on specific problems. We appreciate the opportunity to do business with Disneyland through Art Adler."

Rhino, Inc. T. J. McLarty, President, July 15, 1983: "Thank you for the recent purchase orders placed with our company for rigging repairs to the ship *Columbia*. You will recall that the nature of this work was on somewhat of an emergency basis in that it had to be accomplished prior to the July 4th weekend and we were notified of it on June 27. We wish to comment on the professionalism shown by your office in expediting our efforts to get the facts, get on site, and get going on the job. Your response to our inquiries and obvious expertise in negotiating for an organization as complex as Disneyland made our task much easier."

Bill Pettifer, July 12, 1983: "Thank you for your fine cooperation when I was the lead planner on the refurbishing of the computer and braking system at the Matterhorn. As you recall, there was numerous delays in starting the project and also the weather was not in our favor at times. I feel that one of the reasons the project was finished on time was your cooperation in getting the contractors together on such short notice."

Bert Harrington, July 13, 1983: "I would like to take this opportunity to express my gratitude to you for your help and expertise in handling not only routine jobs, but also very difficult jobs. Your assistance made my job a lot less difficult in working with contractors. It is a pleasure to watch a professional conduct a meeting in a controlled environment, and not allow it to go astray."

I have many more from that time period as well as a huge file filled to overflowing of other records that I kept throughout my decade with Disney. It wasn't all fun and pixie dust, but I am proud that I got the jobs done.

I tell people that the eleven years I spent working for the Mouse were the happiest six years of my life. Yes, the first six years were pixie-dusted magic and were extremely satisfying and productive; I never wanted them to end. Then my eyes were opened and I saw much too much.

Let's start at the beginning.

I have loved Walt Disney, Mickey Mouse, Goofy, and the rest of the gang since I was a kid. To grow up and be a part of the great Disney organization, with all the perks of free tickets, backstage access, and just being a part of the magic, was a dream come true.

I had had a lot of previous experience in similar jobs, and I had no doubts that I could contribute my fair share to making the magic happen.

I came on board at Walt Disney World in late 1973 in the position of a buyer, then I was quickly promoted to the roles of senior buyer, contract administrator at WDW, and finally, senior contract administrator, a title I received when I was sent out west to Disneyland to straighten out some matters there.

In the 1970s, I drove a yellow Toyota with a Florida license plate that read "WDW-1". I was full of Pixie Dust in those early years.

The Disney University at WDW had a high-level orientation program for newly hired salaried employees. The instructors talked a lot about Walt Disney and his accomplishments and that made me smile. We got a great backstage tour of Disney World and a vice president took us all out to lunch.

On the last day, we went to what was dubbed "The Character Zoo", where the costumed characters got dressed and, in general, just hung out. It was in the utilidors (utility corridors that some people refer to as the "tunnel") that run underneath the Magic Kingdom, almost directly under Cinderella Castle.

We were trained how to act as a costumed character and then taken up into the park. Because I was such a big guy, the only character costume I could comfortably fit inside was Baloo the Bear, the easy going bruin from the animated feature *The Jungle Book*.

The costume was heavy and I could only see, somewhat, through the neck of the bear.

I remember a woman and her small child came up to me and asked if she could take a picture of me with her child. I shook my head "yes" because Baloo, like many furry Disney characters, was not allowed to talk; having such characters talk wouldn't sound anything like what their film versions sounded like, and it would break the illusion.

So, there I was, a grown man in a bear costume hugging a kid I had never met and smiling for the picture. I suddenly realized that they could not see my face so why was I smiling like a dummy? I laughed myself silly over that one after the end of my shift.

They gave us a beautiful colored graduation certificate with Disney characters on the border. I still have mine today, because it meant so much to me at the time.

I thought it was all going to be wonderful.

When I was hired at Walt Disney World, there was still a lot of construction going on for what they called "Phase Two" of the Magic Kingdom. They were so rushed getting the Magic Kingdom open on time in 1971 that some projects had to be postponed, but the commitment was to get it all done by 1975.

I don't know if things had just gotten more casual after the passing of Roy O. Disney in 1971 or that not enough attention was being paid to Disney World because it was on the East Coast and all the bigwigs were back in California, but I was shocked by what I found.

I discovered that managers and directors and even some vice presidents would make deals with the contractors and vendors delivering building materials like ready-mixed concrete, shrubs, and trees.

The contractors would deliver part of their loads to WDW and take the rest and rope it off at the homes of WDW executives. Not all of the executives would engage in this unethical activity, but many did. A few built their whole damn house that way or a garage or swimming pool.

When I worked there, I was asked on occasion by various executives to make a good deal on a washer, dryer, fridge, or some other appliance with some of the vendors I did business with on legitimate WDW projects. It placed me in a very embarrassing situation until I told those to whom I reported that I would not do it any longer.

One day, I was sent out to a vice president's home to wait for a locksmith to show up. When I got tired of waiting for this "no show", I left. The next day that executive moaned to my department vice president and I was called into his office to hear about it. My vice president thankfully chewed out the other vice president after I told him what really happened.

Some of the executives felt they deserved these perks because of their position and apparently had been used to getting them for quite some time.

So, Arthur Charles Adler arrives on the scene and immediately starts to enforce the corporate purchasing policy to the hilt. You can be sure that it really upset these guys who were derailing Disney building materials to their own homes.

My immediate boss, Paul Mullee, loved my attitude and policy in this area and on many occasions came to my rescue when some of these freebie types wanted my scalp.

I am sure I gave him acid indigestion many times as he fought to save my butt because he agreed with what I was doing. He was a very unusual and talented purchasing professional whom I admire with all my heart to this very day. He is a man of great professional ethics and character.

I didn't do this because of any holier-than-thou attitude, but rather because it was important to stand for something good and honest. To me, Disney should always stand for something good and honest.

When Paul Mullee was my manager and then was promoted to director of purchasing and contract administration, and his boss had been moved up to vice president, that vice president never took a phone call about any project we were working on without having Paul Mullee sitting right there with him to answer all the questions that might come up.

You never worked for Paul; you worked with him. That's the way he wanted it. We continued to keep in touch after I left Disney.

One of Paul's great innovations was a purchasing credit card program such as Mastercard, Visa, or American Express with an established gross limit and individual purchasing limit that would save time and paperwork in placing purchase orders. It also saved money!

One day, I was having a problem with one of the contractors I had hired to do some work at one of the attractions. They screwed up big time and were causing me a lot of grief.

To officially acknowledge the screw up, I decided to write them a letter.

Paul always wanted to approve any letters I sent out, not just because he was my boss but because he knew I could sometimes be overly aggressive and uninhibited, attributes not in keeping with the Disney image.

I composed a fiery letter that was anything but in the Disney image, even using some profanity and threatening to kick their "damn butt" if they ever again set foot on Disney property. I had my secretary type it up on WDW stationery and put yesterday's date on it. I put it on Paul's desk while he was on the phone.

All was quiet until he hung up and suddenly he was standing in my office doorway with an ashen, white face and wide eyes.

"Art, you didn't send this out already, did you?"

I told him of course I had because time was of the essence to resolve the matter and that he was too busy on the phone.

When I thought he would pass out, I finally told him it was all just a prank. Then I handed him the actual letter, which was very businesslike and proper.

To this day, we still laugh about that incident and several others. Paul never failed to back me up when I was right in my decisions, and I tried not to place him in uncomfortable situations.

One of the biggest failures of any purchasing system, including Disney World's system back in those days, is when salaried or even hourly employees think they can obligate the company to a contractor or vendor through by-passing the Purchasing Department.

When the invoice comes in and there is no purchase order to cover it, accounting calls us. Guess who gets to go after those who did that and, long after the fact, compel them to generate an approved requisition, which is like pulling teeth?

The only time I would not follow the corporate purchasing policy was when an authorized member of upper management would write me a letter over his live signature directing me to deviate from that policy.

In my ten years with the Disney organization at Disney World and Disneyland, I never have received such a letter, and therein lies the rub, as it were, which gave my boss ulcers.

A little-known fact is that an off-property motel around the corner from Disneyland in the 1970s was owned by Disney. It was called the Heidi Motel.

Originally built by an outside investor, it was somehow acquired by Disney in the late 1960s. It operated under Disney ownership as a motel no one knew was owned by Disney until it was finally demolished in the 1990s to make room for Disney's California Adventure. The northernmost section of the motel is currently the boarding area for Paradise Pier's California Screamin' roller coaster.

The back of a classic postcard of the hotel advertises:

> Heidi Motel. 815 West Katella, Anaheim, California. Thirty-one singles, doubles, and family units—Beauty Rest mattresses—Free TV—Refrigerated air-conditioning—Coffee shops and Restaurants near. Heated Pool. Two Slides. Cabana and Hi-Fi.

By 1991, Disney owned eight aging motels around the perimeter of Disneyland property so that one day they could use the land to expand and build another theme park. These motels were operated through a private management company and looked pretty much the same as when they were first built to take advantage of tourists who wanted inexpensive accommodations within walking distance of the park.

A Disney director, who was always overstepping his authority in obligating Disneyland to an invoice for work by-passing the proper procedure, had authorized the services of an exterminator to get rid of a termite problem at one of those motels.

The invoice was handed to me to straighten out. This director and I got into it, and he threatened to come to my office, which was in the second floor of the warehouse at Disneyland, and knock my block off.

I would not budge on the corporate purchasing policy, and I told the director to pay for the service out of his own pocket. He never did show up to knock my block off, although I waited for him.

Eventually, after much deliberate delay, I wrote the requisition myself, got it approved, and the vendor was paid, because we did have a fiduciary responsibility to do so.

I still felt that part of the problem was also the vendor's in that purchasing professionals should never accept a "go ahead" for work without a purchase order number that can only be issued by a purchasing agent or a buyer, not a director.

Months later, this Director's son was caught stealing merchandise from the warehouse and was fired and prosecuted. Like father, like son, when it came to being ethical and following the rules, I guess.

When I flew up to Montreal, Canada, in the late 1970s to negotiate a contract for the automatic turnstiles at the main entrance of Epcot with the Automatique Corporation, it was a real experience for me.

I flew up on Canadian Airlines. I was flying first class, and when I identified myself to the crew as a Disney Cast Member on a business trip, I got to go and sit in the pilot's cabin and watch the nose of the big jet bob up and down like it was threading a needle.

Once in Montreal, I was introduced to smoked meat and great whole pickles in a big jar, and Canadian beer. They treated me like a king, but got nothing in return from me except a damn tight contract with no gravy.

Then there were the days I did some undercover work for the WDW Security Department, since I was a friend of the manager and he knew how much I loved acting and was good at it. They used me from time to time on investigations they were conducting.

Once, I had to act like a typical father going to rent some Disney films at a store in Tampa for my child's birthday party. The store owners had been illegally pirating Disney films. I rented the movies, which were not legally available, and gave them to Security. The store owner was arrested and his store closed down.

On another case, I was asked to watch a certain director who would go to the Men's Store in the Contemporary Resort and steal expensive ties. I was dressed as a typical Disney tourist, but the times when I was there to observe him, nothing happened.

In my most unusual case, I was asked to watch a certain director having sex with his secretary on an old Chinese junk floating in the Seven Seas Lagoon near the Polynesian Village Resort.

I took up my position at the Eastern Winds, a cocktail lounge aboard an authentic sixty-five foot Chinese junk docked at Disney's Polynesian Village Resort from 1971 to 1978. The junk was available for charters and took a crew of two to operate; a pilot and a deckhand. The ship included a galley on board for dining as well as a full wet bar.

Why that director decided to have his little encounter on that particular watercraft is beyond me. My friends in maintenance would tell me that they were never able to get a distinctive stink out of the ship ever since Disney first bought it.

Now, the process I used at my regular job was fairly simple, but I think even a brief summary would be pretty boring to the casual reader of this book. However, for those who might be interested, here is a quick overview.

Basically, I set in place that the bigger the project, the higher the dollar value, I would invite more companies to bid. I often went to former bidders in specific areas that had proven themselves. For new bidders, I checked credit ratings and bank references, former customers, and the contractor's licensing board for any complaints and violations.

I would put together a project team" and select a project leader. I would schedule an Invitation to Bid (ITB) meeting with drawings and specifications. We would all sit down in a conference room and do a job walk-through with the project team and the potential contractors. Then a sealed bid was required.

If, for instance, there was a major electrical rehab project, it would be all electrical work, and so I would only bid the scope of the work out to pre-qualified electrical contractors.

However, if in addition to the major electrical work, there was also concrete work, re-bar, excavation, and some mechanical work (plumbing and pipes, pumps, valves, and such), I would probably go to a pre-qualified list of general contractors to bid the scope of the work, and they in turn would deal with the other trade contractors or sub-contractors as the general contractor.

At the specified time, the bids were opened and we would select the apparent low bidder. Even then, we double-checked to see if there were any errors or omissions, and if there were, the contractor got a chance to submit a revised bid.

If it was higher than the next lowest bid, we went to the lower bid.

Any changes that were required during the course of the work were added to the contract within the cost estimate by mutual agreement. After the final inspection when the work was completed, the contract was closed out and the final payment made.

This process turned out to be efficient, devoid of favoritism, and cost-effective. It was so successful that the company transferred me to Disneyland to implement it there.

When I was promoted to senior contract administrator and sent out to Disneyland, I was told I was there for the specific task of implementing the procedure I just described so as to avoid some of the same issues I had originally encountered at Walt Disney World.

Because Disneyland was so entrenched with its operating traditions, I was told that what I was expecting to do could never be accomplished, or at best it might take up to five years to make all the necessary changes.

I accomplished it in six months.

Bob Penfield, one of the original Cast Members who had been on hand when Disneyland opened, and who became a good friend, sent me an inter-office memo on July 8,1983:

> You know, I remember a couple of years ago when one of my biggest problems was outside contracts and dealing with contractors. But, alas, the "Thin Man" from Florida arrived and showed us the proper way to do things and now it is almost routine in nature.
>
> I remember many a time on pre-bid walk-throughs that very frankly we, as a Disneyland Team, did not have our act together, but with your guidance (even though the frustration must have been tremendous) you were able to pull the ends together and got us prepared and working as a unit.

While I have been talking about the Disney Company using outside contractors, I do not mean to diminish in the slightest that both Disneyland and Disney World had their own departments, including machine shops, and sign shops, that were filled with very talented individuals who maintained everything on property on a day-to-day basis. They also had the capability of building things completely from scratch when necessary.

The only difference between the two shops was that Walt Disney World was an Open union shop, which meant that hourly employees did not have to join a union, and. Disneyland was a closed union shop, in which hourly employees had to join a union. Salaried employees were never required to join any union.

No matter where the Disney Company physically moved our offices in Purchasing and Contract Administration, there was without fail one framed piece of artwork that was always hanging in my office in plain sight.

No, it was not a photo of a smiling Walt, although that was there as well.

It was a large framed picture of the long-haired Abominable Snow Man that had been placed in the Matterhorn with his growling fangs and black face with blood-red, angry eyes, and reaching out menacingly with his clawed hands.

I had a Disney sign painter add these words at the bottom of the framed picture: "WHAT DID YOU SAY? YOU WANT AN EXTRA ON THE CONTRACT?" It sent a clear message that anyone dealing with me needed to follow the proper procedures and that it would be very difficult to get adjustments after the contract was approved.

I still have that framed picture and, as a matter of fact, I am looking at it right now as I write these words.

Hanging on to that picture was a priority for me. One time, Paul Mullee called me into his office before they moved our department from the Casting Building into a warehouse facility.

He was a little sheepish when he said, "Art, I don't really know how to tell you this, but the decision has been made above me that you will be limited to no more than ten Disney items to post on your office walls."

Granted, my office looked like a packed Disney museum, but I still asked, "Why, Paul?"

He said that some of the other purchasing staff felt intimidated and uneasy when they had to come into my office. Of course, you can't really argue with your boss's boss, and the decision had been made. I liked and respected Paul and didn't want to give him any more trouble than was necessary.

But I was not shy telling him what I thought of that decision and the reason it was made!

So, I packed up most of my treasures, which included a hand-drawn sketch in black marker of the Mad Hatter by Disney animator and Imagineer Bill Justice.

At one time, I had quite an extensive collection of Disney memorabilia. Some of it I donated to the Walt's garage display. Some of it I gave away to friends. Some of it I sold to raise money for the many charities I am involved in. As I have gotten older, I have sold off most of collection so that others can enjoy it as I did.

I did keep in my office my white construction hard hat that I always wore on construction sites whose contracts I was managing. On the front it had Mickey Mouse stretching a dollar bill and underneath that picture it read "Art Adler".

Purchasing and Contract Administration is a very sensitive area because it is our responsibility to spend money. We are not selling anything, whereas Food and Beverage and Merchandise Purchasing are doing their jobs for re-sale and profit.

So, the only way we have to make the bean counters in Finance happy is to save money by coming in under the budget and/or estimated costs on original contract awards and any subsequent revisions and change orders that may follow.

Even when a contract for an attraction is completed and the ride is a huge hit, it will eventually wear out over time from use. Then the attraction has to go through rehabilitation (rehab) and it comes back to my department for another set of contracts.

When I was working at Walt Disney World, some of the maintenance contracts I personally handled included:

- Construction of the first huge bird aviary at Discovery Island near Fort Wilderness Resort

- Repair of the Fort Wilderness Railroad tracks and ties

- The new Big Thunder Railroad attraction

- Painting of the exterior of the Polynesian Village Resort

- Purchase and installation of the wave machine in the Seven Seas Lagoon near the Polynesian

- Leasing of the two huge cranes to hold the Epcot emblem in the air for the ground-breaking ceremony by Disney officials and four living Florida governors on October 1, 1979

- Purchase of the new electronic and automatic turnstiles for Epcot from Automatique in Montreal, Canada

- All Wellpoint, diesel generators and pumps, and construction equipment rentals and leases

- Rehab of the Tea Cup Attraction

- Re-painting of "it's a small world"

- Construction of some tree houses at Lake Buena Vista Shopping Village Area

- Major roofing repairs on multiple attractions

- The re-modeling of a few restaurants in the Contemporary Resort

I also did some preliminary work on developing sources for an automated electronic warehouse store and pick system for Merchandise. My promotion to Disneyland in California interrupted that process.

Disneyland was built on limited acreage which precluded any major expansion projects that would occur regularly at Disney World. At

Disneyland you had to literally tear down one attraction to build another, as was the case with the New Fantasyland in 1983.

Most of the projects I worked on there were MRO projects (Maintenance, Repair, and Operation). My primary role was to bring the corporate purchasing policies in line with what I had developed at Disney World.

Here are some of the contracts I personally handled at Disneyland:

- Re-roofing of Space Mountain
- Computer braking system on the Matterhorn
- Fantasyland rehab project
- Rigging the Sailing Ship *Columbia*
- Roofing projects
- Guest parking lot re-paving
- Temporary Fencing contracts
- Heavy equipment rentals and leasing

I enjoyed doing these jobs and others like them until I left the company in 1984. My philosophy mirrored that of Roy O. Disney when he dealt with contractors and outside vendors: firm but fair.

While I was "thrifty" whenever I could be, I realized that a reasonable price and a reasonable profit must be allowed to contractors if I ever expected them to bid again on Disney projects. I just tried to establish that Uncle Scrooge's famous money bin with its unlimited treasures was something found only in Fantasyland and not backstage in the Purchasing and Contract Administration.

Twelve

Other Memories of Working at Disney

I have many memories of working for the Disney Company, but so much has happened over the last twenty-five years that it is difficult to remember all of them until something prods my aging brain.

Here are a few that came to mind while I was writing this book.

Strike Out

There was a maintenance employees strike at Disneyland in late September 1984, and I still have a strike poster in my possession.

One day, I went out to see the strike line because I had friends in maintenance who were hourly. I saw four or five guys in dark suits wearing dark glasses wearing fedora to try to hide their faces as they were hanging around on the outer perimeter of the action. I said to a friend I was with that they must be union goons. He replied that they were just Disney management checking things out.

A few days later on my return from lunch, I had to drive through the strike line, so I brought some snacks for the strikers. I was observed doing that and was called on the carpet for it as an executive giving aid and comfort to the enemy!

Don't Judge a Book by Its Cover

One day I washing my hands in the men's restroom at the Walt Disney World Casting Building, where the first Purchasing Department offices were located back in the mid-1970s.

A stall door opened behind me. Out came the director of Human Resources, the most meticulous man I have ever met, with his perfectly combed hair and pristine suit, just like he stepped out of a Sears and Roebuck Catalog. This guy breezed right out the door without washing his hands. I never shook his hand ever again when we met!

My Main Street Window

Most guests at Disney World and Disneyland now realize that those names on the second-floor windows of the stores on Main Street, U.S.A. are the names of people, usually salaried and management types, who made significant contributions to the parks.

My name is not up there on a window. One day, a friend who worked in maintenance suggested to me that, as a lark, he was going to have a window painted with my name on it. He did and it was fun for awhile, until someone wised up and had it taken out. I never heard one word about it either, which I guess is a good thing.

Food for Thought

Three of my favorite places to eat and drink at Disney World were at the Polynesian Village, Resort, the Empress Lilly, and Cap'n Jack's.

One of the restaurants at the Polynesian served a huge round of beef that they would carve off in front of you nice and rare, with great gravy and mashed potatoes. I would eat four big plates in one sitting and then charge it on my Disney credit card.

The Empress Lilly (named after Walt Disney's wife), a stern-wheeler river boat, served a huge, frozen glass bowl with a stem filled to the brim with ice-cold beer along with homemade potato chips made fresh right on board. I cannot even remember how many beers and baskets of chip I would consumer there with my pals from Purchasing after work.

Also at the shopping village was Cap'n Jack's. They served bouilla-baisse in a crock bowl that blew your mind. It was made with clams, shrimp, crab, and fish, mixed with vegetables, herbs, onion, tomato, leeks, garlic, saffron, fennel, orange peel, and bay leaves, all served together in a hot clay crock bowl with toast rounds. My mouth is watering just telling you about it. It was fantastically delicious!

Bob Snow

I know this is heresy, but there were some great places outside of Disney World property. One such place that I enjoyed tremendously was Rosie O' Grady's Good Time Emporium, opened by Bob Snow in 1974.

It had singing bartenders, can-can girls, and an eight-piece Dixieland band. It was known for nickel beer nights, street parties, and dancing waitresses who served fancy drinks, such as the Flaming Hurricane, in souvenir glasses.

Snow was a clever guy and quickly expanded into other restaurants and shops into what was known in a few years as the Church Street Station area, which became Florida's fourth-largest tourist destination, attracting 1.7 million customers per year.

At the time, I was writing a column of entertainment news called "Entertainment Plus" for Orlando's *La Femme* newspaper. I knew Bob Snow and we got along just great as long as I gave him good reviews, and when I did, he deserved them. I got plenty of free meals and drinks. He was a very handsome, flamboyant guy. He sometimes lived in a private railroad car near the railroad station.

Disney saw his great success and tried to copy it by building Pleasure Island, but it wasn't even close. However, Pleasure Island did succeed in killing Church Street Station, so it was gone before the 1990s ended.

Hurricane Preparedness

In the 1970s, there were many a Florida hurricane or severe tropical storm that threatened the Orlando area, including Disney World property. With one of them coming, Disney was looking for volunteers to stay at our Purchasing offices in the warehouse complex. I volunteered because I was single.

That evening when it was supposed to hit, I sat at my desk by the phone with a two-way radio to Security to call in any damage reports. Earlier in the week, it had been my responsibility to arrange for rental emergency equipment to be on hand, including diesel water pumps, diesel generators, and a few small cranes.

I came prepared with a battery radio, some food, and a thermos filled with vodka and tomato juice, otherwise known as "Art's Famous Bloody Mary" just in case I had to keep warm.

It was the only time I ever brought an alcoholic beverage onto Disney property and drank it there. It tasted good about 3:00 a.m. in the morning. The destructive hurricane never materialized; lots of very high winds and heavy rain. No damage that I could see in the dark. But the Bloody Mary tasted great and made me feel great. After all, it could have been my last drink had the hurricane hit!

Fashion Statement

While I was still working at Disneyland, I portrayed as a union actor the role of the evil and angry King Herod the Great in the world-famous *Glory of Christmas* pageant at the Crystal Cathedral Church.

I was so convincing in my role that it bothered me somewhat because the children in the audience got too scared. After each performance, the cast would stand outside and greet the audience, and I saw that the children were afraid to even look at me.

It really bothered me. So one night, I put on one of my many Disney Mickey Mouse t-shirts under my Herod costume. When a child came near to me looking afraid, I would open up the front of my costume and flash my Mickey Mouse shirt. The look on the child's face would change to a happy smile immediately. Every season, from that night on, I wore that Mickey Mouse shirt!

The Money Truck

The only gasoline-powered vehicle back in my day allowed in the utilidors at Disney World was the Brinks armored truck that came down into the tunnels with only inches of clearance to spare to pick up the daily cash from Cash Control. All other vehicles were battery operated for environmental and safety purposes.

Shields and Yarnell and Adler: Christmas at Disney World (1978)

There always seemed to be something filming on Walt Disney World property.

Robert Shields and Lorene Yarnell were a popular husband-and-wife performing team who specialized in doing comedy mime and dance. They performed on stages worldwide, as well as on countless television and film appearances. They even had their own television show in 1977.

That probably explains why they were chosen as the stars of the December 10, 1978, televised special, *Christmas at Walt Disney World*.

The basic premise was to show off the wonder of Disney World when a robot couple (played by Shields and Yarnell) called The Clinkers decide to visit the park. Both Shields and Yarnell performed other roles as well, like Pinocchio.

The show also featured Phyllis Diller, Avery Schreiber (as Geppetto), Danielle (from *What's Happening!!*) Spencer, Andrea "Annie" McArdle, Pablo Cruise...and me!

There was an ad in the *World-Gram*, a WDW employee publication, asking for extras and character actors to appear in the special. Of course, I showed up.

When I arrived, there were two-hundred-and twenty-five people there and at least eight for the role that I really wanted, a typical Disney World tourist.

But I was the only one who came prepared. I was dressed in white slacks, blue shirt, red jacket, white straw hat, rose-colored sunglasses, and an enormous cigar with both a camera and binoculars hung around my neck.

I had seen so many tourists that I knew what to bring. That did the trick and they said, "You've got the part!"

I was surprised when they brought out W-2 forms; as a salaried Disney Cast Member, I didn't think I was going to get paid. I received $350, which was union scale (minimum payment for an actor in this type of part).

The day we taped the show was November 14, 1978. I arrived for taping at 11:30 am, but didn't go before the cameras until 4:30 p.m. That's the way it often goes in the television and film business.

It was only a forty-five second scene and we rehearsed it twice before the actual taping began. Shields told the director, "Hey! We're wasting our time rehearsing. This guy's fantastic!"

In my scene, I am sitting on one of Disney World's benches on Main Street, U.S.A., reading a park map, smoking a stogie, and eating popcorn all at the same time.

Shields, dressed like Pinocchio, is being chased down the street by Keystone Kops. Pinocchio stops because he is curious about the tourist and his cigar. He takes the spare cigar in my pocket.

I twist off half the cigar in Pinocchio's mouth, popcorn flies all over, push comes to shove, and Pinocchio goes flying after I snap his bow tie.

It was a wonderful bit of physical humor, typical of the great motion picture comedies.

It took twenty minutes for them to do three "takes" of the action because everything had to be reset after each take.

The most marvelous thing was not being on television and telling my friends and family to watch—it was that the experience reawakened an interest to do more acting, something that had been stirring inside me since I was a young man.

I used the opportunity to join the entertainment union AFTRA (American Federation of Television and Radio Artists). On one of my business trips back to California, I made time to visit the Disney Studio and get information about casting and agents.

I was especially prodded to do so by all the enthusiastic comments I got from other people who saw the show.

Robert Shields was warm, friendly, and unassuming. He wanted me to be just as good if not better than him in the scene.

I always remember that graciousness.

Much later, I got to be in a photo session for a large poster for Tokyo Disneyland in English and Japanese. I was on the *Mark Twain* riverboat as one of the passengers on the upper deck, wearing much the same "Florida Tourist" outfit that had gotten me the role in *Christmas at Walt Disney World*: white pants, solid blue shirt, solid red sport coat, and a white Panama hat with a colorful hat band.

You can see my short scene with Robert Shields/Pinocchio on YouTube. It begins at the 0:57 mark:

http://www.youtube.com/watch?v=IoSgHa_db6o

Fourteen

Meeting Celebrities at Disney

As you might suspect, many celebrities visit the Disney theme parks. Here are a few that I remember meeting personally.

Jimmy Carter

President Jimmy Carter came to visit Disney World to speak to a group of people. He was going to appear inside the Magic Kingdom in the archway of the castle. They planned to bring him up through the utilidors. First, the Secret Service and Disney Security removed all the garbage cans along the path and welded shut all the metal manhole covers, among other excessive security measures. I made sure through my friends in Disney Security that I had a spot right next to the door that Carter and his wife were coming out of near the castle.

It was Jimmy Carter's birthday that day or that week. I was standing next to a Secret Service Agent and he warned all of us, "Whatever you do, do not make any sudden moves toward the president!" Well, President Carter comes out and I got right over to him and shook his hand saying, "Happy birthday, Mr. President!" The Secret Service agent almost passed out, but Mrs. Carter said, "Oh, isn't that sweet?"

Were I to try something like that today, I imagine my career (and maybe my life) would be cut short.

Royal Dano and Ernest Borgnine

Strangely, I met Royal Dano, the actor who voiced the Audio-Animatronics President Lincoln at Disneyland and Disney World, not in the parks, but through the Masons.

I met him as part of my Masonic Shrine work at Al Maliekah Shrine Temple in Los Angeles when he and fellow Shriner (and 33rd Degree Mason) Ernest Borgnine asked me to perform a dramatic patriotic piece at the then upcoming Grand Lodge Communication at Nob Hill in San Francisco.

Peter Ustinov

In 1976, the film *Treasure of Matecumbe* was wrapping its final scenes at the beached shipwreck on Discovery Island near Fort Wilderness Resort. One of the stars was Peter Ustinov. I took him out to dinner one evening at one of my favorite Disney World dining spots, the Polynesian Village Resort. I got autographs from the entire cast, including Robert Foxworth, Joan Hackett, and Vic Morrow.

On the way over, I took Ustinov to see my office in the Casting Building. At the time, it was filled with over two-hundred-and-fifty pieces of Disney memorabilia. Ustinov joked that I should install a turnstile outside my office and charge admission.

Vic Damone

One evening after a night of eating and drinking at an Annual Salaried Employees Christmas Gala at the Contemporary Resort, and feeling pretty happy as I got into the elevator, I saw this guy standing inside and started to stare at him because I knew that I knew him from somewhere.

In my slurred speech, I asked him: "Don't I know you from somewhere?"

My purchasing supervisor was with me and he said, with the same slurred speech, "Knock it off, Art. You don't know this guy."

I said that I knew I knew him. All the time this guy and his date were laughing like hell, and then it dawned on me who he was—an extremely popular singer of that day, Vic Damone. One of the best in the business, right up there with Frank Sinatra

I blurted out, "Hey, you're Vic Damone. You're as great as Sinatra!" I asked him for his autograph and he gave me one. That's when my supervisor and I realized we had gotten out on the wrong floor.

Herb Edelman

Some people may remember Herb Edelman for his work on the television shows *Golden Girls* and *St. Elsewhere*, but he had a huge list of television, film, and stage credits. When he was in town performing in the play *The Odd Couple* at the Bob Carr Theater, I got him into Disney World and took him down into the utilidors under Cinderella Castle.

He loved it so much that he gave me a secret password, "Damon Runyon". He said whenever I wanted the favor returned, all I had to do was say that password to him and, if possible, the favor would be granted.

It really worked. When I relocated to California, I used the password to get acting tips and lessons from Herb at his house in Malibu.

Michael Iseberg

Michael Iseberg used the stage name "Michael Iceberg" and was a hugely popular entertainer at Disney World and Disneyland in the 1970s and 1980s. At Disney World, he performed at the Tomorrowland Terrace, where Cosmic Ray's Starlight Café is currently located.

He played a very unusual musical instrument called an "electronic synthesizer monster". The music was fantastic!

Michael and I had many conversations after I got off work about his unusual musical instrument and how he had dreamed up such a contraption. To me, the amazing thing about all of this is how he remembered all the keys, buttons, and switches which surrounded him, making it necessary for him to turn from left to right, and sometimes entirely around, to play this unique instrument.

He was literally surrounded by Moog synthesizers and other electronic gizmos and then all this incredible music came out like from another planet. The Disney guests totally loved him, a real musical Rube Goldberg.

Fifteen

RCID

The Reedy Creek Improvement District (RCID) is so important to Walt Disney World, but little understood by the general public. In fact, I don't know if I fully understand it.

When it came time to build Disney World, the Disney Company needed plenty of flexibility and also consistency. The building codes in Orange and Osceola Counties were inconsistent and, of course, never covered building such things as a nearly two-hundred-foot castle or multiple flying elephants.

The Florida Legislature created the RCID in 1967 and gave it the authority to handle things like road construction, utilities, emergency services like medical and fire, building codes, waste treatment, and a lot more.

So, Walt Disney World is like its own little city or county with full authority to do whatever it deems necessary.

As I understand it, there is a five-member Board of Supervisors that act for the district in terms of making decisions. Each member owns an undeveloped five-acre lot of land within Disney World.

There are two "towns" populated by Disney employees or their immediate family members: Bay Lake, with about two dozen residents and located on the north shore of Bay Lake itself, and Lake Buena Vista, with about sixteen residents located right up the street from the Saratoga Springs Resort.

This is all done to meet legal requirements for such special taxing districts.

When I worked at Disney World, the RCID administrator was Tom Moses. He had succeeded in 1974 the first administrator, General Joe Potter. I worked a lot with RCID and got to know Tom very well. He was a sharp guy with a lot of responsibility. He was also the minister of music at his Baptist Church in Pine Castle and directed the adult choir.

I used to jokingly call him The Governor.

A native of Virginia, Tom Moses came to Florida to be director of building and planning for Winter Park in the 1960s. He is partly Native American. When I asked him about it, he smiled, "Cherokee, about three generations back, on my mother's side. How you link up 'Moses' with that, I don't know."

One of the most interesting and fascinating things at Disney World when I first arrived on the scene in late 1973 was the two large jet engines at Reedy Creek that generated much of the electric power required on the property at that time.

They told me that they cleaned the jet engines by running crushed walnut shells through them. The shells were abrasive enough to clean off the carbon build-up but not harsh enough to wear away or damage the jet engines.

Over in that same RCID backstage area behind the Magic Kingdom were these huge water cooling towers which provided the cool water for all the air handlers in the attractions, because using air conditioning would have pushed the operating and maintenance costs right through the ceiling.

If a guest looks closely to the left from the Magic Kingdom train before the curve heading to the new Fantasyland station, they might catch a glimpse, except that the buildings are painted a light sky-blue color to blend into the background.

One of the other top people working under Tom Moses was a retired military colonel named Tom Jones. A very pleasant fellow and I really liked him. He was a high-energy kind of guy and put a lot of power behind his voice. His office was at the actual power plant site.

Another great fellow was Bill Williams, who worked under Jones. When Bill retired from Disney World, they conducted meetings with a Disney management committee, as they did with other retirees back then, to make a determination whether Disney would pay off on any pension. Bill got caught up in that mess, but eventually was awarded his rightful and deserved pension from Disney. This policy was changed by the Florida Legislature soon after that, and so this situation no longer happens at Disney.

Sixteen

It Takes People

"You can design and create, and build the most wonderful place in the world. But it takes people to make the dream a reality."

Those were the words of Walt Disney, who said so many equally profound things that we still refer back to them today.

Both Disney World and Disneyland were wonderful places, but what made them work, what allowed them to provide magic and happiness for so many people, what made them so memorable, *were* the people.

There are many amusement parks in the world, but guests come to Disney parks because of the people who work so hard to make the magic a reality, often without recognition.

I want to turn a spotlight on some of these names that people don't know and tell their stories. There were some pretty terrific but unknown people on the Disney payroll.

Ed Campbell

Ed headed up Disney's own Buena Vista Construction Company, which handled certain construction and maintenance jobs. They also supervised, on behalf of Disney, the outsourced major construction, rehab, and maintenance projects which was the area where I spent most of my time bidding and administering. Ed was a friend and a down-to-earth Florida native who really knew his business and shared his expertise with me.

Bud Warner

Bud was another purchasing manager during my time at Disney. He was a tall, lanky, mature ex-Marine and professional purchasing talent. Bud was manager of the MRO Section (Maintenance, Repair, and Operation). A real no-nonsense fellow.

Bud was a devoted family man who lived in Windermere and had three sons, one of whom was special needs, and one daughter. His wife was a principal at a special needs school. After Bud retired from Disney World, he became very sick and soon passed away. Bud's special needs son eventually got a job at Disney World and actually retired from there. I have huge respect and admiration for Bud Warner.

Orlando Ferrante

Orlando joined Walt Disney Imagineering in 1962. Over the course of his forty-year career with Disney, he oversaw the installation of the first Audio-Animatronics show in Disneyland, supervised the installation of attractions at the 1964 New York World's Fair, established a department he termed PICO (Project Installation Coordinating Office), and supervised show and ride installations for every theme park built by Disney during his tenure with the company. In his final years, he supervised the installations in Disney cruise ships.

His formal WDI title was vice president of engineering, design, and production.

To say that he only "supervised" installations would not be correct. Orlando was a hands-on person who worked side by side with the people physically doing the work at all times of the day and night.

A former star on the University of Southern California football team and later a guard for the San Diego Chargers, Orlando still looked like he'd be a formidable opponent on the line, many years after his retirement from professional football.

My early encounters with Orlando were not the best. I think he resented this guy from Florida coming to California and getting heavily involved with their purchasing activities.

A turning point in our relationship came, I believe, one day in his office when I stood nose to nose with Orlando and did not back off in a disagreement we had over some issue. I always remember Hank Dains, the director of the Decorating Department, tugging on my arm pleading with me to back off in fear that Orlando might deck me.

He did not, thank goodness, and when I think back through the years and the many occasions I worked with him in trying situations, I never recall Orlando losing his temper. You would know when he was angry, but I never heard him shout at anyone. Everyone respected him.

I am proud to say we became friends.

Al Ross

Al is a gregarious, humorous fellow and a good friend with whom I have had a lot of laughs. He worked in the MRO (Maintenance, Repair, and Operation) section of the Disney World Purchasing Department.

We used to have the greatest times after work at The World Inn or aboard the Empress Lilly River Boat at Disney's Lake Buena Vista Shopping Village. They had the best "Happy Hour" around. Al and I are still in touch regularly.

I asked him to tell me about his Disney Career in his own words. Here it is:

> After four years in the US Navy and ten years at Martin Marietta, I applied at Walt Disney World and was accepted as a purchasing expediter. This was in early 1971, the year that Disney was to open the Magic Kingdom. After one year, I was promoted to assistant buyer, and three years later I became a full buyer.
>
> In mid-1980, I was promoted to senior purchasing buyer with a great team under my leadership. In late 1980, I became a purchasing supervisor responsible for overseeing the purchase of building materials such as plumbing, electrical, and electronics, just to name a few. My last promotion was early 1990 as one of the five purchasing managers where I remained until my retirement in 1994.
>
> I remember as a young boy always buying the Disney comic books and now here I was working for them. I think the "pixie dust" really hit me the day I played Winnie the Pooh. As part of the Disney training I had to be in character and interact with the guests at the Magic Kingdom. Boy, was that costume hot!
>
> I never had a chance to meet Walt Disney himself, but I did get to meet his brother Roy. I have always had the feeling that if Walt Disney ran the country we would be better off.
>
> One of the many things I will always remember was Cross Utilization or, as we called it, Cross U.
>
> The salaried staff would work in the park running the attractions and food venues. I remember one time working with a co-worker, Art Adler, at a food location in the Magic Kingdom making hamburgers.
>
> We were told any broken burgers coming off the conveyor belt should be tossed in a large pan to be used for chili at a later time. Then I noticed that Art was eating them instead! Never a dull moment with Art Adler.

Being on the ground floor of the Walt Disney World Company was very exciting for me. During my twenty-three years with Disney, I made many good friends, both co-workers and vendors alike. I can think of nothing I would change except for staying in better touch with everyone.

After Disney, I worked for a local plumbing supply company as a sales representative for two years and then thirteen years for a brochure distribution company in public relations. I had plans to work with my brother, Bob Ross, a well-known TV artist. Bob had wanted to do a children's TV program, but sadly enough Bob passed away before his dream could be realized.

Today, I reside in Ocoee, Florida, with my wonderful wife, Sheila, of 25 years. We have two daughters (his and hers) and four beautiful granddaughters. God bless our troops, America, and Mickey Mouse!

Al Ross mentioned the WDW Cross Utilization Program where salaried employees had to take a regular hourly shift or a day in some different department not just to help out but to get a wider perspective of the business. It could be anything from operating a ride to janitorial (what we called "potty patrol") to just handing out maps at the front of the park and giving directions.

I always tried to get assigned to working in food and beverage because I would eat well; all those broken hamburgers that they would use for chili never made it to the pot whenever I worked that station. I looked upon it as a perk!

Al tells the story of a guy who robbed the Contemporary Resort, and while he was running away from the crime scene, he ran head-on into a tree and knocked himself out. That made it much easier for Disney Security to catch him. It was the way Al told it that always had all of us laughing.

Costumed Disney Characters

The Disney live costumed characters are worth every penny they are paid and more. It is a hard job, maybe the hardest of all, due to the energy that is required. They can only stay out walking around the theme park for short periods of time because it is so physically taxing with the Florida heat and the weight of the costume.

They also put up with a lot of abuse; while the guests do see them as "real" characters, they do their jobs so well that people don't think there is a real human being inside. They get pushed, punched, and tackled, even with another Cast Member out there to help them.

Parents get angry when the characters have to leave for a well-deserved break.

Walt Disney told his executives that it is the Disney characters that make the experience different at a Disney theme park. He reminded them that guests, no matter what age, light up and smile when they see them in the park.

I was only in a fur costume for a few hours as part of my orientation training. They did that for executives back in my day because it gave them a real perspective not only in the difficulty of the role but in how the guests reacted to it. As much as I love acting, I wouldn't want to do that job.

Facilities Department

These craftsmen and artisans were among the best natural or developed talent on property. They were incredible and could paint, build, repair, change, make signs, design, create, and take on almost any task and produce a quality product. Every single time.

Costume Department

Everything used to run and operate a Disney theme park must be repaired or replaced at some point in time because they just wear out from use and touch. The Costume Department had to handle thousands of different costumes from the characters to the people who worked in the rides and shops and restaurants and elsewhere. They did it all, every day of the year, and they did it so well that we sometimes take it for granted.

Seventeen

Bob Bowman:
My Dance with Disney, 1971–1996

My friend of later years, Bob Bowman, retired in 1996 as vice president of Retail Procurement of Character Merchandise for Walt Disney World and Disneyland.

Bob worked for Disney during all of my ten years with the company, but we never met. However, I heard many positive things about him from my former boss, Paul Mullee. It was Paul's passing on my political emails, "Eagles Nest USA", that connected Bob Bowman and myself about four years ago, and now we are close friends as well.

He lives in Orlando and I am seventy miles away from him in Mims, but we get together from time to time to chew the fat about Disney and politics over a steak and a few drinks.

Bob had also tried to write his own book about his Disney career called *My Dance with Disney: 1971-1996*. I asked him if he would like to share a little of it in my book, and here is that excerpt:

"I always marveled at Walt's vision for family entertainment, the quality he insisted on that is still maintained today. He inspired all of us to seek the best quality in any product we created that was exposed to guests (the general public).

"It was in 1968 that I returned from Vietnam as a staff sergeant and was stationed at the U. S. Strike Command (now called Central Command) in Tampa, Florida. One year later, I decided to leave active duty for the Marine Corps Reserve.

"While serving in the Marine Reserve beginning in 1969, I was attending school at Embry-Riddle Aeronautical University full-time and working full-time in retail at Montgomery Ward in Daytona Beach. In the early summer of 1971, I decided to take a photo sales job traveling north Florida, but the territory was not opening up until January 1972.

"In the interim, I decided to apply for a photo buyer position at Walt Disney World, but heard nothing back from them after several weeks.

"During one weekend drill around August 1971, I ran into a reservist who was in my reserve unit and reported to me. I was giving him a lot of crap about missing drills only to find out that he not only was given special permission to miss drills but that he also was an executive involved in retail merchandising.

"I mentioned to him that I had applied at Disney but had not received a response to my resume, and he asked me to send a copy to him. The executive was Ed Moriarty, one of the three directors who came to Florida to open and operate the merchandise shops at Disney World.

"Within a couple of weeks, I had an interview with Disney. However, I was a little disappointed and didn't anticipate it when they told me the photo buyer's position had been filled a few days previous.

"They then offered me a sales job at $2.05 per hour. I immediately turned it down, and the interviewer stepped out to call someone. While he was gone, I had a conversation with myself and it went like this: 'Why did you turn down that position when you have nothing to do for the next four to five months while the photo sales territory and job becomes available?'

"I decided right then I would take this job, and then when the sales job opened up, I would give my notice and leave. In the meantime, I could eat.

"I started working for Disney World in September 1971, pricing film in the warehouse and doing odd jobs until the park opened on October 1, 1971. I was then promoted to a senior sales host making $2.15 per hour.

"In late November 1971, Disney fired the person they had hired for the photo buyer's position. When I found this out, with bravery, I called up Ed Moriarty and told him I wanted to interview for that position, which was what I had originally applied for.

"He called me a few days later and said he would set up an interview with Jack Olsen, the VP of merchandising, who would make the hiring decision.

"In early December, I had an interview with Jack which lasted about 30 minutes. My resume showed that I had a pilot's license, so for the first 25 minutes of my interview we talked about flying because he, too, was a pilot. Then suddenly he said, 'Now why am I talking to you? Oh yeah, you are interested in the photo buyer's job.'

"He pulled out his Nikon camera from his desk drawer, pointed to the depth of field scale on the lens, and said, 'I have always wondered how this feature works.' I began to tell him exactly what the scale was for, and he then put the camera back in his desk and said, 'You're hired.'

"I thought, 'Gee I really taught him something.' Come to find out later, Jack knew more about cameras than I ever would in a lifetime.

"From that point on, I was involved not only buying for the Main Street Camera Shop but was also its operations supervisor. As time progressed, I was relieved of the supervisor role and worked full time in the Buying office.

"I later took on additional buying responsibilities, such as Disney character watches, which Jack Olsen was very interested in. Jack wanted to design a Mickey Mouse watch with Bulova, because our contractual watch company, Elgin/Bradley, did not have the quality Jack wanted.

"So I got to work with him personally in introducing the very first Bulova Mickey Mouse watch.

"Later in my career at Disney, around 1978, I switched categories and was buying for decorative gifts, primarily for Adventureland.

"After a couple of years in that role, my general merchandise manager, Tony Schroeder, promoted me to be his assistant manager of the Buying offices for the Magic Kingdom, hotels, and campground.

"In 1982, Tony asked me to consider going to Tokyo Disneyland to take a director's position to oversee Merchandise Operations and Buying there. I was hesitant to take the job at first, but my senses came to me over the weekend and I accepted.

"I have to say it was the best decision of my Disney career, because I was exposed to many upper-level folks in my two years in Tokyo. It was a distinct pleasure working with my Japanese counterparts to open 39 merchandise shops in just twelve months from the time I arrived.

"I enjoyed going back in April 2013 for the 30th anniversary and seeing all the folks I had worked with 30 years ago. I have a deep affection for the Japanese and the warm and sincere acceptance and appreciation they showed me while working with them.

"I did have one challenge over the quality of merchandise we would allow in Tokyo Disneyland. When I arrived in March 1982, thirteen months prior to park opening, not a single piece of merchandise had been developed.

"So, my first priority was to get them going on designing and developing merchandise for the park. After sitting through several minutes of a meeting in which they were showing me merchandise that they wanted to sell in the park, I stopped the meeting.

"The merchandise was of the quality you would find in the early days of Japanese junk items. That was their idea of what they thought would be appropriate for an 'amusement park'.

"I spent about thirty minutes telling them how Walt insisted on quality, no amusement park stuff, and that the merchandise should represent the quality experience guests would have in the park and then they would want to take a quality souvenir home with them, etc.

"They all listened very intently, or so I thought. Great, they know what I'm looking for. So we proceeded with the meeting. The next item presented was the same; another cheap-looking piece of junk. I knew I had to get their attention.

"I asked the staff sitting on the opposite side of me to please open the windows behind them. It was about 35 degrees outside, so they hesitated and said if I was too hot, they would turn the heat down. I insisted on the windows being opened.

"By now, there were several of these 'junk items' on the table. One by one, I started throwing them out the window to the ground. They were trying to catch them as I threw them. My words were, 'We are never going to sell this junk in Tokyo Disneyland.'

"They got the message and, henceforth, they designed and produced some of the best merchandise in any of our parks.

"After returning from Tokyo in 1984, I was in a merchandise manager position at the corporate headquarters in Burbank, responsible for all the Cast Members who were buying the Disney/character merchandise for Disneyland, Disney World's Magic Kingdom, and Epcot.

"After one year in that position, I had an opportunity to work with the Purchasing Department, taking a director position supporting the Studio in Burbank, WDI Design Group in Glendale, and Disneyland.

"I enjoyed my tenure there of four years and left in 1989 to transition to director of Purchasing at Walt Disney World, reporting to the same vice president.

"Ten months later, the company reorganized the Retail Merchandise Division and asked me to take over as vice president of Retail Procurement of Character Merchandise for Disney World and Disneyland. We moved the office from the Studio in California to Florida and hired an entire new staff to consolidate all the buying. I retired as a vice president in 1996."

Bob Penfield: The Last Original Disneyland Cast Member

Bob Penfield headed up Area Supervision at Disneyland while I worked there. In many respects, he was the counterpart to Ed Campbell at Disney World. Bob was the last original Disneyland cast member to retire from working at the park.

When first I was promoted to Disneyland as senior contract administrator to clean up and standardize the purchasing and contract process as I had done at Disney World, it was only through the dedicated support I received from Bob Penfield that allowed me to eliminate the corruption of my predecessor.

Bob and I are still in touch, and I am very grateful for his support and expertise.

He is a straight shooter, and I liked him right off the bat when I arrived at Disneyland back in 1980. I sensed Bob felt the same way about me because we share similar political beliefs, and he is a big fan of my "Eagles Nest" political emails. He has even sent me material that I have included in them.

He was a terrific associate who would lay any criticism he had about any pending decision I was making out of ear-shot of others on the project team.

Bob told me that he met Walt Disney for the first time in 1959 while working on The Jungle Cruise about four years after being hired, just before the grand opening of Disneyland.

He had conversations with Walt several times after that about the attractions and how to improve them. Bob said that Walt would regularly sit down and have coffee with an attraction Cast Member to get their feelings on how things were going and the guests' reactions.

I asked Bob to tell me the story about how he came to the Disney Company and about his successful career there. Here's what he said:

"I started to work at Disneyland on July 13, 1955, four days before opening. I had just turned 18 and graduated high school, and it was my first real job, the only job I ever paid taxes on. Before that, I had only worked on a farm at a dollar an hour. Disneyland paid $1.65. I was in heaven.

"I was a ride operator assigned to Fantasyland, specifically the Peter Pan ride. Because so many of the rides were not ready, we trained on others, plus test rode many in other lands.

"I also was assigned to George Whitney, who was in charge of the construction and implementation of Fantasyland. He would have me run around Fantasyland with messages to other personnel, plus at times over to Adventureland, which I did not even know where it was. I had to ask.

"On opening day, it was a total mess.

"We were asked to come in early as the traffic was expected to be terrible. Ray VanDeWarker picked me up and we parked below the eucalyptus trees on the old Winston Road that was later called the Ball Road Gate. At the time, I think it was just the North Gate.

"The park didn't open until the afternoon and coverage proceeded to each land with the television special ending up at Fantasyland. I was scheduled to be on the Peter Pan ride, but it was not ready so I was moved over to the King Arthur Carrousel. We had more than enough help, as many of the rides such as Dumbo were not completed yet.

"The Storybook Land ride at that time was known as the Canal Boats of the World and was basically just the canal with nothing on the banks, mostly weeds, some of which were marked as to what kind of weeds they were.

"They were operated by all-male operators and used Johnson 10-horsepower outboard motors which were inside the aft compartment. They would vapor lock constantly and had to be towed into the storage area. The operators actually discouraged the guests from riding, but they still wanted to.

"When the drawbridge was lowered, all of the children came rushing in, climbed over the chains around the carousel, and overwhelmed us. We had to shut down the ride to keep control. Another thing was that we were really learning our roles on the job that first day.

"Later on, we had a gas leak and the area had to be cleared, but it was minor.

"After three days, I was made foreman of the afternoon shift of the Snow White ride and had mainly school teachers and young Marines from Camp Pendleton working for me.

"During the first two winters, I went to college and worked the late shift getting in 40 hours most of the time. I decided to make Disneyland my career and progressed up through the ranks in the Operations Division. I was assigned to the 8th Winter Olympics in 1960 in Squaw Valley to help Disney with the operation of the games. In 1964-65, I was assigned to the New York's World Fair at the Pepsi Cola Pavilion, 'it's a small world', for a total of eight months.

"In 1966, I transferred over to the Maintenance Division spending two years in Custodial, then ten years in Maintenance Services as the superintendent, then ten more years in the same position in Area Supervision.

"I worked for three months in Florida helping to open Walt Disney World in 1971. I was later assigned to Tokyo Disneyland for nine months in 1982–83. Upon returning, I took over the Roofing Dept., then moved into Construction Services and Project Management, where I retired in 1997 after 42 years of service.

"I am a member of Club 55, a group of the original employees, and there are now only 17 still alive. I was the last member to retire from Disneyland.

"My only connection with the park now is that I am president of the Disneyland Anaheim Breakfast Club (ABC), which meets once a month and holds special breakfasts at the park's anniversary and again at Christmas, when we usually have 80 attendees."

Nineteen

Paul Mullee: My Boss

Much of my success at Walt Disney World was due to the support and help of my boss, Paul Mullee. I have already praised him several times in this book, and I wish I could shower him with even more praise.

He was everything a Disney director should have been. He was passionate but even-tempered. He was ethical. He backed up his subordinates, often when it would have been easier not to do so, especially in my case.

When he first notified me that I had the position of senior buyer in the Disney World Purchasing Department and gave me a start date in late 1973, I decided to take a short vacation before beginning work.

I drove up to Gatlinburg, Tennessee, a real fun place in the Smoky Mountains everyone should visit at least once. While I was there, I bought one of those novelty newspapers where you can have the front page headline changed to whatever you want. Mine read: "Arthur Adler Famous Actor and Purchasing Agent Takes Position at Walt Disney World Co!" I mailed it to my new boss for laughs, and Paul did laugh. It was one of many laughs Paul and I would share over the rest of our lives.

I wanted Paul's story in my book because of the huge impact he had on my Disney career. Here it is, in his own words:

"I well remember the thrill I experienced on a phone conversation in December of 1970 when I accepted a position in the Purchasing Department at Walt Disney World. At the time, I was the purchasing manager at the Microelectronics Division of the Philco-Ford Company in Lansdale, Pennsylvania, after having been a supervisor in Philco's corporate office in nearby Philadelphia.

"Working for Disney, in addition to enabling me to continue a career of over sixteen years in corporate purchasing roles and doing so with a world-renowned and respected company, would make my daily dream and longing to return to Florida come true.

"The person in charge of purchasing for Disney World was Roy Noblitt. I had been Roy's mentor when he joined the purchasing department at Martin-Marietta in Orlando in the early 1960s, and we became good friends.

"Roy and I kept in contact through my moves to Detroit, where I worked for a leading design-build firm, and while in Pennsylvania. After joining Disney, Roy said he would like me to consider working with him there, and he would contact me when there was a need to expand the department.

"Being a man of his word, Roy followed through, arranged for my interviews with several executives during Thanksgiving week of 1970, and I started work at Disney World on January 15, 1971. And so began a wonderful chapter in my life for me; my wife, Ada; and my young children, Pam, Paul, and Greg.

"My initial responsibilities were to head the contracted services section of the department as well as the procurement and rental of all capital equipment. In other words, my job was contracting for any and all services, construction or otherwise, and I was quick to learn that the volume of requests would be huge.

"Purchasing for Disney World was either a buyer's dream job, from the aspect of the variety of products and services that had to be purchased, or a buyer's worst nightmare, based on that same aspect.

"You had to be prepared to buy things you never imagined you would be asked to buy.

"For example, and this is a story I enjoy telling, I received a requisition to purchase flamingos, thirty of them, I believe, to eventually be located by the hotels.

"The request stated Argentinian flamingos, but the primary importing agent, located in Miami, told me that there was a quarantine on Argentine flamingos, but he could obtain Chilean flamingos, which were similar but their color faded more as they aged. I laughed and told him our paint shop would find a way to handle that.

"Then he asked if I wanted their wings cropped. I asked what would happen if they were not cropped. 'They will fly.' 'How far?' I asked. 'All the way to Chile,' he replied. 'Crop them,' I said.

"There are many, many stories and experiences that come to mind when I think of the twenty-three plus years of my tenure with Disney, but my first thoughts are of the outstanding Disney people who impacted my life.

"A few months after the grand opening of Walt Disney World, a decision was made by the VP of the Finance Department, to whom Roy Noblitt reported, to place the man who had managed the purchasing effort for the Contemporary and Polynesian hotels, Howard Roland, over Roy.

"Howard had left an executive purchasing position with Sheraton Hotels to take on the effort at Disney. His buying knowledge and abilities and his strong business acumen became apparent during the construction of the hotels to management on both coasts.

"Unfortunately, Roy could not adjust to the change. He, too, had done a good job, and he could not accept that he was no longer the manager of the department. Within a few months of the change, Roy submitted his resignation and left the company.

"I felt badly about Roy's leaving, but had known for some time before his resignation that the relationship was not going to work. His frustration and unhappiness was very obvious. I would miss his presence and will always be grateful for his having made it possible for me to work for Disney.

"I found Howard easy to get along with and quickly recognized his keen business sense and his ability to go to the heart of problems and seek and offer solutions and make firm decisions.

"I also learned fast that he would be very annoyed when I, or anyone, would repeat information that he already knew or was long-winded in explanations. I always knew when I slipped up on either of these points. I liked Howard, and we got along well together.

"Howard had garnered the respect of the very top executives in Disney's corporate offices in Burbank who had, by the way, been very active in the development of Disney World and had traveled and spent much time in Florida. They were definitely hands-on and important in every aspect of building this complex project.

"Howard interfaced very well with these executives and eventually the move was made to promote Howard to a corporate director level which gave him the purchasing responsibilities on both coasts and later to the position of vice president.

"My responsibilities and positions rose as well, first as WDW's purchasing manager, and then in December 1980, during construction of Epcot, as director.

"I have occasionally been asked over the years if I had ever met Walt Disney. Regrettably, Walt passed away in 1966, but not before being the major figure in identifying the specific area in central Florida where he wanted Disney World to be built.

"I did have the great pleasure of meeting Roy O. Disney, one of Walt's brother, shortly after the opening of Disney World. Roy was another 'giant' within the company and well-respected in the business world in general.

"He served as the Walt Disney Company's first CEO, its chairman of the board from 1945–1971, and its president from 1966–1968.

"Roy was a soft-spoken man who shunned publicity and went out of his way to avoid having his picture taken. From all that I was told, Roy was a warm and well-liked man whose guidance of Walt in their many endeavors was hugely valuable.

"The orientation program that I went through when I first joined Disney included many film clips of Walt. Some of them were never seen by the public. These films made the man very real and alive to me. He was a person you liked immediately. In spite of all that he had accomplished and his marvelous personal talents and his worldwide fame, he was still humble and warm and caring.

"A second extensive orientation program that I was fortunate to qualify for took place perhaps a year later. It included ten days visiting Disney's West Coast organization, which included the Studio in Burbank, WED/MAPO in Glendale, and of course, Disneyland.

"Touring the facilities was exciting and informative, but it was the people we met, many of whom spent considerable time telling us about their roles and what their departments did, that made significant impacts on us. They left us without any question that Disney strove to provide the best in every venue they were in, and to provide the finest in family entertainment.

"A number of the people who sat with us were themselves well-known worldwide as artists, sculptors, designers, and architects who had worked directly with Walt for years, and they provided much insight into the man.

"The West Coast orientation included a dinner at the home of Donn Tatum, a man little-known to the public but whose long-time contributions to the company helped make it what it became. Donn, for me, was the warmest, kindest, most likable gentleman of high corporate ranking that I have ever met.

"The evening with him and his dear wife was delightful and one I will never forget.

"Donn joined the company in 1956 and remained active on the board of directors until 1992. His quiet leadership during those years encompassed such high-level positions as president of Disney World, CEO of the Walt Disney Company, and chairman of the Walt Disney Company.

"The first corporate officer I was personally introduced to was Card Walker, the Disney CEO from 1971–1983.

"I remember saying, 'How do you do, Mr. Walker?' and quickly, but warmly, being told that his name was Card. Here was a man who went from being a mail-room clerk to the highest position in the company, but was unpretentious and immediately put me at ease.

"My wife and I would later have the experience of flying from Orlando to Burbank on *The Mouse*, the corporate airplane. On the flight was Card and his wife and Jack Lindquist, another Disney legend who spent thirty eight years with Disney in positions that included director of marketing and, from 1990–1993, president of Disneyland.

"On at least two occasions on the flight, Card came to the area of the cabin where Ada and I were seated to be sure that we were comfortable and had enough to eat. His actions were genuine and that's what I learned to like about so many of the Disney management people. They truly cared for others.

"When I think of outstanding management people, Dick Nunis quickly comes to mind. Walt Disney World opened on time thanks to this man. I do not believe any other person could have accomplished what Dick did.

"I can still see him every day walking the construction site with his hard hat in place and a portable phone in one hand, a tape recorder in the other, leading a group of people, some of them stumbling on the rough construction site trying to keep up with him while taking notes as Dick spoke.

"He was an untiring dynamo who solved many problems on the spot, identified other problems requiring action, assigned action to be taken, confronted contractors with their problems, and did every-thing else humanly possible to get the job done, properly and on time.

"What a guy he was! He also saw to it that Disney employees and their families were recognized for their efforts and the sacrifices they made in order to get this Herculean project done. He brought us, children and all, to the job site on more than one occasion and would often personally lead the groups through the various 'Lands'.

"In his long career with Disney, Dick served as the first vice president of both Disneyland and Disney World, and also as the chief operating officer.

"I spent approximately five years on the Euro Disneyland project with the same responsibilities that I had at Disney World: purchasing, contracted services, warehousing, and traffic control.

"I started traveling to Paris every other week from Orlando from January of 1988 through June, when my wife and I became the first family to relocate there from either of the two U.S. parks.

"We were fortunate to reside in a lovely three bedroom, two-and-a-half bath, fifth floor apartment on rue Castiglione in Paris.

"A wonderful location! The famous Ritz Hotel in Place Vendome and the old Opera House were a few minutes walk in one direction and the beautiful rue Rivoli, the Tuileries Gardens, the Louvre, and the Seine River were short walks in the opposite direction.

"Outstanding ethnic restaurants were within walking distance from our apartment, and although most of them were not two- or three-star restaurants, they were more affordable and, by our standards, provided some of the best food we had ever eaten.

"Although twelve hour (plus) working days were the norm for me at Euro Disneyland, I took advantage of the weekends—until the last several months prior to opening day when weekends became regular work days—and Ada and I traveled by car and saw much of France, northern Spain, England (via the Hovercraft), Holland, Belgium, Italy, Germany, Switzerland, Austria, and Luxembourg.

"It was a wonderful experience, and I am very grateful to Disney for having made it possible.

"I had two previous foreign assignments many years ago, the first being in Madrid, where I was a buyer for a joint venture of three major U.S. construction companies on the building of air and naval bases in various locations throughout Spain.

"After that, I accepted a purchasing agent's position with another joint venture of U.S. and Canadian companies on a road and bridge construction project in South Vietnam and we resided in Saigon. This was in the late 1950s, prior to the war.

"Approximately thirty years later I took on the assignment in France for Disney, and it would become the most memorable experience of my life. A most demanding and stressful job. In addition to the long hours, cultural adjustments that had to be made both in everyday living and in our business efforts, including formal adjustments in our legal purchasing and contracting conditions.

"I was, by some formulation or other, allowed to have on my staff two other Americans. I chose to transfer a young man, Roger David, with contracting experience in our WED/MAPO Purchasing Department in Glendale, and was fortunate to be able to hire Bill Cook, a gentleman with extensive experience in purchasing for hotels. Bill had just completed a foreign assignment for the Marriott Corporation and was eager to extend his experiences overseas.

"Bill became my manager of what is referred to in the business as the FF&E section of the department (furniture, fixtures, and equipment). This section purchased everything for the park and the five hotels and campgrounds, including wallpaper, draperies, art work, and all the components that went into hotels—pillows, sheets, bedspreads, dishes, flatware, glassware, and so much more.

"Roger became the manager of our contracted services section which handled just about every service that we did not perform with our own personnel. And that list was extensive.

"I hired two men from local businesses to become managers of our food buying section and our central purchasing section, the largest section within our department, and the one which purchased everything that was not bought by the specialized sections.

"Stephan Berly headed the food buying and food preparation and kitchen equipment procurement. Stephan came with extensive knowledge of food and equipment after having worked for years at a prestigious major French corporation.

"Alain Leonard, pronounced like 'Lay-o-nar', a high-level purchasing executive for one of the largest construction companies in France, became our manager of the Central Purchasing Department.

"The purchasing effort for this project was a huge effort. The variety of products and services required and in the volume we needed were mind boggling. For many of them, there were no existing companies with the capabilities or capacities to handle our needs. So we cultivated them.

"For example, the dry cleaning business in France had some years before become a cottage industry, what we would refer to as 'mom-and-pop' businesses. Large facilities to handle very large volumes did not exist. This applied to uniform supply companies as well.

"After extensive research and effort, we were able to encourage the larger companies in these fields to agree to expand their facilities. We were able to get competition for the work and eventually awarded the largest dry cleaning and uniform supply contracts ever awarded to French companies.

"We accomplished similar purchases for our bread and pastry needs, causing new facilities to be constructed or expanded to meet our needs.

"One of our most meaningful accomplishments, which is still saving a great deal of money for the company to this day, is one that I doubt anyone in Disney management has ever recognized and that we purchasing guys were quietly proud of—the customs agreement that we negotiated with the French government.

"It was another of those exhaustive negotiations that took several months, but the results, with favorable classifications of materials and equipment and favorable tariffs, would result in saving us millions of dollars under what we would have otherwise paid. The French favored us with a trade agreement that an American lawyer working in this field for years in France said he never thought could be obtained.

"I give a lot of credit to the then manager of WDW's Traffic Department, John Killingsworth, whom I brought over to France several times to guide us in this effort, as well as to establish shipping guidelines for our Purchasing Department. John was the most knowledgeable man in his field.

"I can say with conviction that Disney was a great company to work for. The company expects a lot, demands a lot, but it gives back a great deal. It is good to its employees and to the families of its employees.

"I still say, with pride, that 'yes, I worked for Disney'.

"There are so many other names of memorable people that come to mind, but I hesitate mentioning some for fear of overlooking others and regretting it later. However, since this book centers on the life and times of one Arthur 'Buddy' Adler, especially as they relate to his Disney experiences, I would be remiss not to tell you something about Art, as I always addressed him.

"As departments expanded and space within the Magic Kingdom became limited, I was asked to arrange for the relocation of our

Decorating Department from the theme park to leased facilities in Orlando. I solicited bids from major moving companies in the area and set up a pre-bid walk-through with the companies' reps so that they could get a feel for the magnitude of the move.

"So, representing one of the firms bidding the job, here comes this big guy who looked like he could be playing on the line for a professional football team, dressed in a bright orange blazer and black pants, as tan as a man could get, and grinning from ear to ear. He introduced himself as Arthur Adler. I liked him from the moment I met him.

"As it turned out, Art's company was the low bidder and I awarded the job to them. Subsequently, Art came to the park to look at another job, and he asked me if there might be an opening in my department. Art had considerable previous purchasing experience, and I was on the brink of getting approval to hire another buyer, one who had contracting experience. Art seemed to fit the need perfectly, and very soon after our discussion, he started work at Disney World.

"Art quickly became an asset to the department. He was an excellent contract administer and a hard worker.

"He also started to qualify as the most unforgettable character I ever met and would become a cherished lifelong friend!

"He was a man of many talents and interests, as well as being a humanitarian. I burst out laughing every time he did his pantomime of the announcer in the Spike Jones recording of the auto races and his rendition of Louie Armstrong's 'What a Wonderful World', complete with trumpet in hand.

"What I would like to add is that there have been untold numbers of what I refer to as 'Disney's unsung heroes'. These are the people who work behind the scenes. These are the people who are not 'onstage', so to speak. They rarely receive public recognition, but their extraordinary efforts and contributions made it all happen.

"The Imagineers, the people who create and engineer the shows, the designers, the artists, the architects who design the buildings, the decorators, all—and rightfully so—get their names in print and are acknowledged for their accomplishments.

"The spectacular show makes one forget all that goes into making it happen. I can tell you first-hand that the exceptional efforts of thousands of people behind the scenes is required during the construction of a theme park and the critical need to meet the opening date previously announced to the world.

"Every work discipline you can think of is stressed. Finance department, computer services, the landscape people, the entertainment techs, the people who sew the costumes, the communications people, the personnel in the shops (painters, carpenters, fiberglass specialists, and mechanics for every type of vehicle you can think of), purchasing people who were always under the gun to bring in supplies and equipment to meet critical schedules, and so many others.

"We were all Cast Members, not simply employees of the company. Those of us Cast Members who worked backstage impacted the end results and that affected our guests.

"I was fortunate to have worked for some outstanding companies in my forty-year career in purchasing, but the years with Disney were the best."

Twenty

Walt Disney and Me

Even though I never met Walt Disney, he was always an inspiration.

I certainly felt his presence when I first set foot into Uncle Robert's garage. The inside had never been painted or coated with anything. It was raw wood. I stared at that bare wood and very hesitantly and gently touched it. Had Walt touched that very same spot?

When I relocated to Disneyland, I immediately knew that it was different from the more spectacular Disney World because I could sense Walt Disney's karma. I could feel his presence.

If I were to come up with one word that describes Walter Elias Disney, it would be "dreamer". I have been a dreamer, too, for most of my adult life, so I can understand and appreciate the process of dreaming. Being a dreamer is much like being in love, in that there is always a chance it will not work out and you must be prepared for that.

Fortunately, for both Walt and I, most of the things we dreamed did become a happy reality. We both had a dream standing in that little old garage.

He was an American icon and a force for good and happiness in this world. Even though he is gone, he remains alive in our hearts and mind. He will never be forgotten.

Walt was not perfect and certainly had the same human shortcomings that we all do. He could be a hard task-master or, as my father used to say, "a tough man to shave".

Yet, even though he has been physically gone for half a century, he continues to inspire and bring great joy through his many creations to both children and adults. His final legacy was giving us the gift to dream of a better world. He certainly reflected God's will that we should all have hope and should strive to be the best we can.

I hope that if Walt Disney had known me, he would have liked me and the way I got things done, even with all my imperfections.

When I picture Walt, I always see him smiling.

Twenty-One

Now It's Time to Say Goodbye!

I often get asked if I loved Disney so much, then why did I voluntarily leave the company after close to eleven years?

I explain that I needed to put in a full ten years and a little more in order to be vested in the retirement program to receive all the benefits. That is true.

It is also true that I would have loved to have worked there longer. I thought I did a great job and made a significant difference, and I loved many of the people that I worked with. I loved almost every other minute.

I was employed doing a job of making children and adults happy.

I also loved the perk of telling people that I worked at Disney. I loved getting people into the parks, sometimes even backstage, and taking them to see the massive Disney memorabilia collection in my office. At Disney World, I would arrange to use my free tickets, and any tickets I could get from my friends who worked there, to take abused children from the Melbourne Children's Home into the park to go on the attractions and meet the characters.

As a salaried employee, the Disney Company provided me with a good salary (and some very nice raises), benefits (including life insurance and hospitalization), a Disney credit card, an allotment of all "E" ticket books (back in the day they still used ticket books), stock options, sick days, two weeks paid vacation, a credit union, an annual Christmas gala for salaried employees that would blow your mind, employee discounts, and two great secretaries (Rose Mortimer at Disney World and Lucinda Lucia at Disneyland).

But no company or corporation is perfect. If you work long enough for them and rise fast enough within them, you come to know things that maybe you would rather not know or have experienced.

The Disney Company after Walt's death moved in a different direction because other personalities with other plans for the future took over and ran things, especially the parks that were bringing in the lion's share of the company's revenue.

A lot of upper management types slowly took more and more control, while claiming to be working in Walt's memory, and started to take it to a place I didn't want to go.

As much in awe as I was working there, especially for the first six years, I could sense something was "off". The business of making a profit, a HUGE profit, was taking precedence over everything else.

There were vicious office politics fueled by jealousy, fear, and resentment that seemed to increase each year and prevented the magic from happening or, at least, from happening the way it used to happen in the days of Walt and Roy.

Especially at Disney World, I saw the "Cult of Original Employees". These were the people who were there from day one and were still in "battlefield mode". In the beginning, things had to be done quickly in order to get the park open, and so policies and paperwork were often bypassed.

The mission was to get the job done no matter what the cost, and there was often no time to look for multiple competitive bids. Do the work and send us the bill. Deals were made quickly just over a phone conversation.

The problem was that after the battle was over, they couldn't switch to a different mindset. They still wanted to do things "the old way".

I'm not saying some of these people did not have talent or did not deliver the goods in a profound way for the success of the Disney theme parks.

Nor am I saying that even the majority were involved in questionable behavior. Yet, they all had the same attitude that I shouldn't be telling them what to do and how to do it. I wasn't a member of the club.

I was told that upper management loved the great job I was doing, especially my aggressive enforcement of the corporate purchasing policy that saved the company millions of dollars over the decade I was there. But I saw that if I pushed too hard, or if someone in that Cult of Original Employees was negatively affected, those same executives would sell me out for less than the cost of an "E" ticket.

There is always a risk in being conscientious, or taking too much pride in your work, or doing what your bosses say they want done but don't really want done. I definitely ruffled plenty of feathers along the way.

People kept complaining, "We never did it that way before!" You could hear the subtext of, "And we don't like it! And we don't like this guy telling us how to do it!"

The reality is that working for the Disney Company was not all pixie dust. I kept mine for many years. For those not familiar with Disney, "pixie dust" is the term that refers to feeling "lifted up", as if Tinker Bell had sprinkled you with dust and you are filled with happy thoughts of doing the right thing and making people happy by doing it.

You can literally see that feeling in the eyes of many of the Cast Members, especially when they first join the Disney Company and go through orientation. Eventually, most people come crashing down to the ground by the harsh business realities, whether it is the unfairness of scheduling, a superior not modeling the proper attitude, or seeing and hearing things that are not what Walt would have wanted.

As I was losing my pixie dust, the thing that kept me going was the memory of Walt himself and what he wanted to accomplish and why. I could see the company was slowly forgetting all of that year by year as bigger and bigger profits became king, often at the expense of guest and cast satisfaction.

Walt's commitment to creating joy, emphasizing quality, and giving the guests everything you could give them were becoming just catch phrases in employee handbooks or monthly meetings and were quickly forgotten as soon as people left the room.

I think the straw that finally broke the camel's back, or at least mine, happened at the end of 1983.

The bombing of the Beirut barracks in Lebanon on October 23, 1983, killed 299 American and French servicemen attached to the Multi-National Force (MNF) during the Lebanese Civil War.

When the bodies were brought back home, American flags were flown at half staff in their honor—except at Disneyland. I was told that we did not want to remind guests of unpleasant things.

When I heard this, I was irate and looked into who made the decision. It was the two Cora brothers, John and Jim, who were top executives at Disneyland and who were Lebanese.

As a military veteran, I was so angry that I wrote a blistering letter to Ron Dominguez, President of Disneyland. I tore into the decision and the Cora brothers.

I felt it was the right thing to do, but I knew that was probably one of the biggest nails in my coffin. I knew I would never become a director of a vice president at Disney if I lived to be 200 years old. A future at Disney was now closed to me.

I could also see the handwriting on the wall that a new administration headed by Michael Eisner was coming on board and they intended to clean house.

Disney announced they were looking to negotiate with salaried employees for an early retirement package. I just had to make sure I didn't do anything until I had a full ten years or a little more so that I was vested in the retirement plan.

I was also eager to pursue a career as a union actor. I had been "bitten by the bug" and felt it would be more emotionally satisfying to entertain audiences than negotiate the lowest possible price for a toilet.

I really don't hold any hard feelings, even though many of my friends have told me it has gotten much worse at Disney than when I was there. Maybe if people like me had stayed and fought, things would be different today. Maybe not.

My legacy at both Walt Disney World and Disneyland was setting a firm but fair process for handling purchasing contracts.

At eighty-one years of age, I am still wearing my Mickey Mouse t-shirt.

Proclamation for Walt Disney Recognition Day

Here is the official proclamation signed by President Ronald Reagan for Walt Disney Recognition Day, which I think should be celebrated every year:

Proclamation 5585—Walt Disney Recognition Day, 1986
December 5, 1986
By the President of the United States of America

A Proclamation

December 5, 1986, marks the 85th anniversary of the birth of Walt Disney. "Uncle Walt", as he was affectionately known to his movie-making colleagues in Hollywood, was just that to several generations of American families: a warm, generous uncle who sat us on his knee and told and retold us stories of comedy, imagination, and adventure. He was a superb animator, a technical wizard, an astute manager and businessman, but above all he was a man who never lost touch with his child's heart and sense of wonder.

Walt Disney's work and the countless characters he created or brought to the screen—Mickey Mouse, Donald Duck, and so many others—are known the world over. But if he is both legend and folk hero today, it wasn't always clear that he was destined to achieve so much. Walter Elias Disney was born in Chicago in 1901. His family soon moved to Missouri, and he worked at a variety of jobs. He returned to Chicago in 1917 and studied photography and art, but he never graduated from high school. After serving in World War I as a Red Cross ambulance driver, he joined an advertising firm in Kansas City as an apprentice cartoonist.

The real harbingers of his future success in this period, however, were the cartoons he produced in a makeshift studio he built for himself above his father's garage. In 1923, he went to Hollywood with $40 in savings and, with his brother Roy, converted another small garage into a studio and set to work. He put together two silent movies with a new cartoon character named Mickey Mouse, but he was unable to get them released commercially. With *Steamboat Willie* in 1928—a sound film with Disney's artwork and his own voice for the diminutive hero's—Mickey Mouse and Walt Disney had an instant hit, the first of many.

Achievements and awards followed in droves. Disney won 30 Academy Awards.

He produced the first full-length animated film, *Snow White and the Seven Dwarfs*, in 1937; launched numerous technical innovations in sound and color; produced the first television series in color in 1961; found new and effective ways of combining live actors with cartoon characters in films like *Song of the South* and *Mary Poppins*; and everywhere, in classic movies from *Fantasia* to *The Jungle Book*, he celebrated the power of delight through music.

The standards of excellence Walt Disney upheld in animation extended to his later productions, from nature films to movie versions of ancient fables, tales of American heroes, and stories of youthful adventure. His love for technology and the future, his desire to entertain and educate, and his sense of childlike wonder led him to establish two popular amusement parks, Disneyland and Disney World, which today draw visitors from around the globe.

Walt Disney's true drawing table was the imagination, his themes were virtues like courage and hope, and his audience was composed of young people—in years or at heart—who, through the creations of this American genius, found new ways to laugh, to cry, and to just plain appreciate the "simple bare necessities of life".

The Congress, by Public Law 99—391, has designated December 5, 1986, as "Walt Disney Recognition Day" and authorized and requested the president to issue a proclamation in observance of this event.

Now, therefore, I, Ronald Reagan, President of the United States of America, do hereby proclaim December 5, 1986, as Walt Disney Recognition Day. I call upon all Americans to recognize this very special day in the spirit in which Walt Disney entertained young and older Americans.

In Witness Whereof, I have hereunto set my hand this 5th day of December, in the year of our Lord nineteen-hundred and eighty-six, and of the Independence of the United States of America the two-hundred and eleventh.

Ronald Reagan

[Filed with the Office of the Federal Register, 2:08 p.m., December 5, 1986]

Walt Disney's Secret Speech

In 1965, Disneyland was celebrating its Tencennial. It was such a large celebration that it was even necessary to create the role of Disneyland Ambassador to assist with all the publicity. It was an exciting time.

The Disney Company had four innovative attractions at the New York World's Fair that would soon be installed at Disneyland, there were plans to re-do Disneyland's Tomorrowland completely, Pirates of the Caribbean was being delayed because of a massive change from making it a walk-through attraction to a boat ride, Walt was already thinking ahead to Epcot and Mineral King, and the animated feature film *The Jungle Book* was in production.

It seemed like the future would be a great, big, beautiful tomorrow, and listening to Walt inspired confidence and enthusiasm that the next five years would be filled with even more wonders, especially for Disneyland.

A special celebration for Disneyland Cast Members was held at the Disneyland Hotel's Magnolia Room on July 17, 1965. For the finale, Disneyland executive Jack Sayers introduced Roy and Walt and invited them to speak.

Walt obviously had some idea about what he wanted to say, but it was not a speech written by the usual Studio publicity people. It was not a formal speech, and Walt wandered over several different topics. As far as I know, the speech has remained "secret" all these years, in the sense that no one has ever played an audio of it in public or put up a transcription of it.

Robert "Bob" Penfield was one of those Disneyland employees invited to the 10th Anniversary Celebration of the Opening Day of Disneyland. He brought along his cassette tape recorder and recorded all of Walt Disney's speech that memorable night. Bob gave me a copy of that tape many years ago when I was struggling to save Walt's first studio to help me keep my spirits up. Bob told me:

The first anniversary of Disneyland to really be celebrated was in 1965, the 10th anniversary, and was held at the Disneyland Hotel, I believe in the Magnolia Room. There were about 500–600 attendees. The booze was flowing and there were a few drunks, one of whom threw up on the back of another.

This was the last time we saw Walt as a group, actually the last time for many of us, as he never came to the park much after that. He died a little over a year later. I would have missed this celebration if I had still been back at the New York's World's Fair, so I guess I can say I was lucky in a sense. Walt was very congenial, as you can tell by the tape.

I wish I could re-create for you on this page the experience of actually listening to Walt because he easily could have had a career as a stand-up comic or an after-dinner speaker. His timing, his choice of anecdotes, and how he told them with the appropriate emphasis on the right word resulted in honest, hearty laughter and applause from the audience.

You miss on paper subtle things like Walt stretching out words like "well" or mispronouncing some words like "acrost" for "across", and you can easily see how he constantly used the word "things" to fill in gaps.

Just try to imagine Walt's introductions from the beginning of his weekly television show and that famous Midwestern twang and rhythm as you read his words.

It was clear that Walt was relaxed and in a playful mood and the encouragement he got from the crowd inspired his storytelling.

I listened to this tape many times while I wrote this book for the inspiration to continue. Listening to Walt's speech always lifts my spirits, and I consider it one of the most valuable Disney items in my collection.

My favorite moment is when Walt tells what I call his "Exotic Weeds" story. Running out of money and time when building Disneyland, he told his head landscaper, Bill Evans, to just put up signs with Latin names near the weeds.

Even just remembering it makes me want to laugh. What an ingenious solution to the problem and one that entertained the guests. I will never tire of listening to it.

For those of you, like me, who weren't there, here is a transcript of that presentation:

Jack Sayers: Ladies and gentlemen, I give you the boss…Walt.

Walt Disney: (clears his throat) I can go back beyond ten years on this deal. I remember a few little things that went on before the opening. I was trying to put a show together for the Golden Horseshoe. Well, I had known Donald Novis for years, and Donald had been around to see me. I said, "Isn't there something we can do? Can you get me a comic?"

And he said, "Yes, I know a fella I was in Australia with. He is getting a little bored living out of a trunk and traveling around the country and the nightclubs…and he might be interested."

I had a little interview over at the Studio. In came this fellow. He had a little bag with him and in the bag he had a dummy. And he had some other things. And he had some bagpipes. He came in there and was on the stage all alone. And I said, "Well, we're trying to put a little show together." I said, "You know this Disneyland, it's going to be a family place." And he said, "Well I have some routines I've been doing in night clubs."

He said, "I can clean 'em up!" (laughter from the audience). And he cleaned 'em up, you know. But I think there's just a little hangover in a few of those little jokes in there, but it kinda slips by and nobody realizes it.

But…that was Wally Boag. Wally, we've been very happy. We hope you stay with us. Wally, I hope you've been happy…

Wally Boag: (from the audience) We're still in rehearsal, Walt.

Walt: (laughing) That's my tag line. You stole it from me.

(Walt talks briefly about Vesey Walker, the band leader at Disneyland, and his son Tommy, who was the entertainment director, but this section is garbled on my tape.)

Walt: I can go back to Joe Fowler. We had to have somebody to really put this together. Someone to take hold of this thing and really make it work. We were told about this retired admiral. He had run the San Diego Navy Yard. The commandant of the Navy Yard who had built ships in China and all of that. And he was starting a subdivision up in San Jose.

So I remember we went up to see him. We went out and met Joe at his home. His lovely wife. We had dinner there. We had steaks. They were wonderful. So we sort of prevailed upon him to come down and sort of be a consultant for us and things. And, little by little, we got him sort of trapped into the thing. We got him so wrapped up in it that he said to hell with the subdivision. I think he owns half of Newport Bay or something now. (laughter)

Well, we had a lot of problems putting this thing together. There was pressure for money. A lot of people didn't believe in what we were doing. And we were putting the squeeze play where we could.

I remember that we were dealing with all three networks…they wanted our television show. And I kept insisting I wanted this amusement park. And everybody said, "What the hell's he want that damn amusement park for?"

And I couldn't think of a good reason except…I don't know…I wanted it. (laughter)

I remember we had a session with NBC. They wanted this Disney television show and we were stubbornly insisting we wanted to start an amusement park with it. David Sarnoff was sitting in on this thing, and he said, "I want your television show, but why the hell do we have to take that damned amusement park?"

Same thing went with CBS. Yeah, they wanted the television show, but the insistence on the backing of this amusement park…

ABC needed the television show so damned bad (loud laughter from the audience) that they bought the amusement park. (laughter and applause)

Well, five years later, my brother figured we better buy those guys out. They had a third interest. They only had a half-million dollars invested in the park.

But my brother figured, "If we don't buy 'em out now, we're going to payin' a lot more later." My brother paid them, after five years, $7.5 million dollars for their $500,000 investment. And it was a smart move that he did it then. (laughter)

Well, my brother has had the worries of getting this money and fighting the bankers and things.

And there was a time, I think it was after we opened the park, that our bankers said to my brother: "Now about that damn amusement park, we're not gonna let you put another nickel in it." And my brother said, "Well, if you're gonna start running our business, we're going out and we'll find some other place we can borrow money." And by gosh, they finally gave him the money.

But it has been nip and tuck. I mean when we opened, if we could have bought more land, we'd have bought it. Then we'd have had control and it wouldn't look too much like a second-rate Las Vegas around here. We could have had a better chance to control it. But we ran out of money. And then by the time that we did have a little money, everybody got wise to what was going on and we couldn't buy anything around the place at all. (laughter)

A lot of people don't realize we had some very serious problems here, keeping this thing going...getting it started. I remember when we opened we didn't have enough money to finish the landscaping. I had Bill Evans go and put Latin tags on all of the weeds. We had a lot of inquiries. (laughter) That's a fact. You ask Bill Evans. Of course, every weed to Bill Evans has got a Latin name, you know.

But at this time...10 years...I want to join my brother in paying thanks to all you people who've been here with us and been a part of making this thing come across.

But I just want to leave you with this thought...that it's just been sort of a dress rehearsal and that we're just getting started. So if any of you start to rest on your laurels, I mean, just forget it.

I've had Dick Nunis on my tail and he says, "You know," he says, "we've got to take care of these people." He's got me workin' harder than I've ever worked before trying to enlarge the park to take care of the extra millions he thinks we're gonna gain every year.

Now...he's got us working hard...honestly. I mean, he says, "Walt, we gotta expand Fantasyland. We gotta expand this"...and he shows me this graph where you started here out with $3 million and the way he's got it going up to $10 million, and he may be right because this year we're just bulging at the seams there.

But do we have plans to expand it...to open up new areas. It's like a sponge. You have to have these areas to absorb the people. And we hope to have these things going.

We have a whole new plan for Tomorrowland. You know, of course, of our plans for New Orleans and eventually the Haunted Mansion. We have a new Fantasyland coming...that'll be next year.

And really, we've got about $40-plus million worth of stuff planned for the next five years. Now...I don't know whether we've got the money to do it with (laughter) but...thank God for *Mary Poppins* out there! (loud laughter and applause)

You know, my office is above my brother's, and I look down, when I see him walking on the ceiling. You know that's the time I go down and say, "Let's put another $10 million in Disneyland." And lately he's been walking all around the ceiling.

Well, I know...are you gonna have some dancing? These boys [the band] haven't done a damn thing all night. They've been sitting over there... on double time, no doubt, huh? (laughter from the audience) And I think that...with just a thanks and appreciation to my big brother... to Joe Fowler...to all the boys...the top boys and all you people down the line, who've been a part of this thing...as I say, we're just getting started, you know. The show goes on next year...Yeah!

As Walt exited, the band played "For He's a Jolly Good Fellow".

A Final Word

It is said that, on average, we all have about 25,000 mornings. That works out to be about sixty-eight years of life.

I am 81 years old as I am writing this book. I have now lived 29,565 plus mornings. So, since I have exceeded the average, I think about just how many more mornings do I have?

That is why it is important to enjoy every morning, because it is not just the beginning of a new day but the beginning of a new chance to make things right, to be open to new opportunities, and to be thankful to God for all his many blessings.

If there is just one thing that I have accepted in this life, aside from the existence of a forgiving and understanding God, it is this: "We all live two lives, the one we learn with, and the one we live after that!"

LIVE YOURS WELL!

Art Adler
July 2014

Art Adler passed away a few weeks before I published his book. It is my great sorrow that he never got to hold it in his hands.

Art was immersed in making the book as good as it could be, and I have over 300 emails and a stack of paper from him to prove his dedication. He sent me one final email after his release from a post-operative rehab center and return home. In true Art fashion, the first line of that email was an inquiry into *my* health.

I will miss Art, his emails, and his bombastic good-heartedness.

Bob McLain
Theme Park Press
September 2014

Arthur C. "Buddy" Adler
May 5, 1932 – September 23, 2014

A Note from Jim Korkis

Arthur C. "Buddy" Adler passed away shortly before this book was published. He had seen the cover and knew that finally his story would be told the way he remembered it.

Art was a force of nature. He was larger than life. He spoke and wrote in capital letters and exclamation points.

He was extremely passionate about religion, politics, acting, his extensive charity work, the United States of America, and of course, Walt Disney. I've known him since 1995 and the heat of those many passions never dimmed even slightly in all those years.

For nearly three decades, he had been working on a manuscript entitled *The Old Garage Nobody Wanted*, about his saving of Robert Disney's garage where a young Walt Disney did his first animation in California. Art attempted it many times, but could never get far enough along to come close to completing the story.

The final impetus came from a conversation between Art and Bob McLain, the owner of Theme Park Press. Bob told Art that if he finished writing his story, he'd publish it. Given a challenge, Art came through.

My contribution to this manuscript was to supply perspective, locate documents, verify information, organize countless news clippings and a myriad of incomplete first drafts, and not stand in the way of Art telling his story the way he wanted it told.

Many people just have supporting roles in their own lives. Art was always the star of his life and never hesitated to promote even the smallest of achievements as if it were fully deserving of front-page attention. He believed in God, country, and perhaps most important, himself. His business card had this quote from Proverbs 3:5: "Trust in the Lord with all of your heart and he will direct your paths."

Publisher Bob McLain and I are thankful we were able to make Art's dream a reality and that, toward the end of his life, he was able to take comfort that his story would finally be told in print for others to enjoy.

Jim Korkis
Disney Historian
September 2014

Selected Bibliography

All of these books helped me to better understand Walt Disney and what was happening in his life when he worked in his Uncle Robert's garage.

Disney, Diane. *The Story of Walt Disney*. Henry Holt & Co., 1957. Walt's daughter tells the story of his life.

Finch, Christopher. *The Art of Walt Disney*. Harry Abrams Publishing, 1973. The complete story of the history of the Disney Company.

Ghez, Didier (editor). *Walt's People*. Theme Park Press, 2014. Fourteen volumes jam-packed with stories of people who worked with Walt Disney.

Green, Howard E. and Amy Boothe. *Remembering Walt: Favorite Memories of Walt Disney*. Disney Editions, 1999. A book of quotes from people who personally knew Walt Disney.

Greene, Richard and Katherine. *Inside the Dream: The Personal Story of Walt Disney*. Disney Editions, 2001. A great book with contributions from Walt Disney's family.

Greene, Richard and Katherine. *The Man Behind the Magic: Walt Disney*. Viking, 1998. A terrific book, especially for young people, to understand the real Walt Disney.

Thomas, Bob. *Walt Disney: An American Original*. Disney Editions, 1994. The first biography I read about Walt Disney and still the best.

Thomas, Bob. *Building a Company: Roy O. Disney and The Creation of an Entertainment Empire*. Disney Editions, 1998. A different perspective of Walt Disney as seen through the eyes of his brother, a very under-rated leader.

Williams, Pat with Jim Denney. *How to Be Like Walt*. HCI, 2004. Great insights from people who actually worked with Walt Disney.

About the Author

Some people don't know who I am. Others know me much too well.

Most people probably know me as the person who saved Walt Disney's first studio, an old garage at the side of his Uncle Robert's house in Los Feliz, California.

It is probably more correct to say that it was Walt's first studio in California. He built his own animation stand which is now housed in an unassuming corner of the California History Hall at the Los Angeles Natural History Museum. Walt himself donated the stand to the museum in 1938 and claimed he had used it to film *Steamboat Willie* after he had upgraded it.

I am proud of what I did, and I don't mind if that is what most people remember about me when I am gone. But there is a lot more to my life, for those who wish to know.

I was born Arthur Charles Adler on May 5, 1932, in Queens, New York. I grew to be six-feet, one-inch tall, and let's say well over two hundred pounds, earning me an ironic nickname by my friends at Disney as the "Thin Man".

I use the name "Arthur" in more formal settings like work and my nickname "Buddy" for my acting roles and more informal occasions. Some people knew me by one name and others by another, so I eventually just used both to identify myself because I liked them both.

I attended High Bridge High School in New Jersey. When I graduated in 1951, I was voted by my classmates as "Most Likely To Succeed".

For over forty years, I have been the founder and sole benefactor of the annual Ethel Ann and Arthur L. Alder Memorial Educational Assistance Award in memory of my mother and father to the High Bridge Middle School with a savings bond to a worthy graduating student. My career highlights include:

1951–1953: American Cyanamid Company in New Jersey. I was a laboratory technician doing pilot plant work using a wide variety of equipment and techniques.

1953–1955: United States Army. I was an ordinance specialist stationed in Vienna, Austria. Honorable discharge at Fort Dix.

1955–1959: Bowen Engineering Inc. in New Jersey. I was a test operator, which entailed the preparation of many chemicals, pharmaceuticals, and foodstuffs in order to process them in the test drying equipment, and I recorded engineering data for design purposes while drying the material.

1960–1963: Nichols Engineering & Research Corporation in New Jersey. I was a test engineer and plant foreman.

1963–1967: American Weldery & Steel Company in New Jersey. I was in complete charge of procurement of materials such as steel, fasteners, hardware, coatings, alloy steel, and office supplies. I was also responsible for keeping all records of the purchasing department accurate and thorough.

1967–1974: Metro Containers (a division of Kraftco Corporation). I was the purchasing agent and later assistant manager responsible for obtaining and expediting materials for complex engineering and construction projects.

1974–1984: Walt Disney World and Disneyland. I was initially hired as a buyer, and then I was quickly promoted to senior buyer, contract administrator, and senior contract administrator.

Senior contract administrator is equivalent to a manager position. I was the first Disney employee to hold that title and was still the only one within the Disney Company to hold that title when I left in November 1984. In fact, I had to write the job description.

It may sound unexciting, but Disneyland's New Fantasyland in 1983 would not have opened on time without my behind-the-scenes help in getting last-minute requests and contractors in place. One of those assignments involved the braking system on the Matterhorn.

A short profile of me appeared in the May 1989 issue of the *Disneylander* magazine. The *Disneylander* was the earliest Disneyland Cast Member publication and first appeared in July 1957. Its primary purpose was to share information about employees like promotions, marriages, births, recreational activities, and similar topics.

I was amused that I was at the top of the list in the summer 1988 issue for a column entitled "Where Are They Now?" People were still curious about what I was doing with my life after I left the world of Disney.

So, I wrote to the coordinator of the magazine, Dianna Stark:

> I resigned from the Disney organization in November 1984 to pursue my secondary career full time—that of a character actor in Hollywood—which I'm happy to say I am still pursuing. I made this career change at the age of 50. It is a difficult, complex business to be in, but performing and moving people emotionally with your acting skills is rewarding beyond measure."

The magazine used that quote and published the following in the May 1989 issue:

> During his eleven years with Disney, Buddy served as contract administrator at WDW and senior contract administrator for new construction and major rehabs at Disneyland.
>
> Since leaving the park, he has appeared in more than twenty television shows and movies, and has done character voices and voice-overs for dozens of radio and television commercials and animated cartoons.
>
> On stage, between numerous other productions, he co-stars (and has given some 800 performances) in annual presentations of the Glory of Christmas and Glory of Easter at the Crystal Cathedral in Garden Grove, California.
>
> But old ties are sometimes hard to break, and over the years Buddy has involved himself with peripheral Disney activities. His most ambitious project was to found "The Friends of Walt Disney", a group of admirers who chipped in enough money to buy at auction the small, old-fashioned, one-car garage which Walt reputedly used as his first studio in Hollywood.
>
> The garage was moved and now stands less than two miles from Disneyland, among other historical buildings at the Garden Grove Historical Society's Heritage Park.
>
> "I really enjoyed most of my years with Disney," Buddy says, "and I've had many happy experiences while keeping Walt's name ever-present in some small way as I work on the projects in his memory. He left a tremendous legacy to the world and the children in it."
>
> Which brings Buddy to The Heather Templeton Children's Wish Fund, the project "nearest and dearest to my heart". In 1982, Buddy learned about Heather Templeton, then nine years old and a victim of cystic fibrosis with rare complications.
>
> "Her wish was to go to Walt Disney World, but she was never well enough to take the trip," he says. So, in 1985, he founded The Heather Templeton Children's Wish Fund, a national nonprofit organization

which so far has granted requests for twenty-five terminally or chronically ill youngsters and assists in paying medical bills.

Buddy helps raise money for the fund by performing *God and Country*, a patriotic and religious one-man show he takes on the road. The organization also gets support from merchants and businesses who give goods and services as well as financial contributions.

"We touch hearts and lift spirits by what we do," he concludes. "It's such a beautiful thing to make a wish come true."

Of course, that profile appeared twenty-five years ago. I have done a lot more since that time.

The Heather Templeton Children's Wish Fund evolved into the much larger Over The Rainbow Children's Wish Foundation, Inc. I served as founder and chairman of the board for twenty-seven years. We have helped children with catastrophic diseases or other illnesses in High Bridge, New Jersey, as well as Brevard County in Florida and Orange County in California.

I was also the sole and founding benefactor of The Angel Award Foundation, recognizing with an engraved glass award and a check those who served their community, fellow human beings, and/or church in some profound manner.

After leaving the Disney Company, I pursued a professional acting career and was a member of the entertainment unions SAG, AFTRA, and AEA.

I appeared in a few small non-speaking roles in commercials and an episode of the Ted Knight sitcom *Too Close for Comfort* in 1983 as well as the movie *Honky Tonk Freeway* (1981) shot in Mount Dora, Florida, near Orlando.

My real love was performing on stage.

I and particularly proud of portraying the role of the terrifying and angry King Herod for the Crystal Cathedral's production of *The Glory of Christmas* and Joseph of Arimathea in *The Glory of Easter* for well over a thousand performances over more than a dozen years. Growing my own long hair, mustache, and beard was no problem when I worked at Disneyland because I was not in the theme park area but worked in an office backstage.

Acting is not a steady source of income so, in recent years, I also hired myself out as an independent purchasing contractor in the electronics industry. I also spent much of my time working for my church and pursuing other interests like model rocketry, where I obtained a Level 3 Certification, the highest level a civilian rocket hobbyist can attain.

I practiced my deep civic and religious beliefs as an active member of the Masons, Veterans of Foreign Wars, American Legion, Jaycees, and as a lay minister of the Crystal Cathedral Church of Garden Grove.

Over my lifetime, I have received countless awards and recognitions in different categories, but one of my favorites and the one that I am most proud of is the medal from the Freedoms Foundation.

On November 16, 1989, I was awarded the George Washington Honor Medal from the Freedoms Foundation at Valley Forge, Pennsylvania, for "excellence in the category of individual achievement" by the foundation's National Awards Jury. Foundation President Robert Miller told me that thousands of nominations had been received that year.

I have led a full and interesting life, and I believe that I made things happier and easier for a lot of people along the way.

And now I've written a book.

About the Publisher

Theme Park Press is the largest independent publisher of Disney and Disney-related pop culture books in the world.

Established in November 2012 by Bob McLain, Theme Park Press has released best-selling print and digital books about such topics as Disney films and animation, the Disney theme parks, Disney historical and cultural studies, park touring guides, autobiographies, fiction, and more.

For more information, and a list of forthcoming titles, please visit:

ThemeParkPress.com

More Books from Theme Park Press

The Vault of Walt: Volume 3

Even More Unofficial Disney Stories Never Told

Best-selling author Jim Korkis brings forth from his famous Vault of Walt two dozen new stories about Disney films and theme parks, Disney stars and attractions, and of course, Walt himself. Disney fans and historians alike will relish these little-known tales.

ThemeParkPress.com/ books/vault-walt-3.htm

The Unofficial Story of Walt Disney's Haunted Mansion

Welcome, Foolish Readers!

Haunted Mansion expert Jeff Baham recounts the colorful, chilling history of the Mansion and pulls back the shroud on its darkest secrets in this definitive book about Disney's most ghoulish attraction.

Foreword by Rolly Crump.

ThemeParkPress.com/books/ haunted-mansion.htm

More Books from Theme Park Press

Disney Destinies

Find and Follow Your Disney Destiny

Karl Beaudry profiles two dozen Disney notables, from Walt Disney and Ward Kimball to Card Walker and George Kalogridis, and traces their paths from delivering news-papers, taking tickets, and washing dishes to the height of Disney fame and power.

ThemeParkPress.com/books/ disney-destinies.htm

Disney's Grand Tour

Join Walt Disney on a whirl-wind tour through Europe at the dawn of Disney's Golden Age of Animation.

Didier Ghez follows in Walt's footsteps on a "vacation" that set the stage for Disney's classic films and influenced everything from Disney ani-mation to its theme parks.

Foreword by Diane Disney Miller.

ThemeParkPress.com/ books/vault-walt-2.htm

More Books from Theme Park Press

Walt's People: Volume 14

What was it really like to work for Walt Disney?

Disney historian Didier Ghez presents the latest in his seminal series of interviews with the Disney artists and animators who worked with Walt. In this volume: Bill Justice, Eddie Sotto, Alice Davis, Admiral Joe Fowler, and twenty more.

Foreword by Todd James Pierce.

ThemeParkPress.com/ books/ride-delegate.htm

Service with Character

Disney Goes to War!

As Hitler's tanks rolled across Europe, the U.S. government informally drafted Walt Disney. David Lesjak chronicles those dark years, when the Army took over the Disney Studios and even Donald Duck went to work for Uncle Sam.

ThemeParkPress.com/books/ service-character.htm

Discover our many other popular titles at:

www.ThemeParkPress.com